twenty

January

S	M	T	W	T	F	S
					1	2
3	4	5	6	7	8	9
10	11	12	13	14	15	16
17	18	19	20	21	22	23
24	25	26	27	28	29	30
31						

February

S	M	T	W	T	F	S
	1	2	3	4	5	6
7	8	9	10	11	12	13
14	15	16	17	18	19	20
21	22	23	24	25	26	27
28						

March

S	M	T	W	T	F	S
	1	2	3	4	5	6
7	8	9	10	11	12	13
14	15	16	17	18	19	20
21	22	23	24	25	26	27
28	29	30	31			

April

S	M	T	W	T	F	S
				1	2	3
4	5	6	7	8	9	10
11	12	13	14	15	16	17
18	19	20	21	22	23	24
25	26	27	28	29	30	

May

S	M	T	W	T	F	S
						1
2	3	4	5	6	7	8
9	10	11	12	13	14	15
16	17	18	19	20	21	22
23	24	25	26	27	28	29
30	31					

June

S	M	T	W	T	F	S
		1	2	3	4	5
6	7	8	9	10	11	12
13	14	15	16	17	18	19
20	21	22	23	24	25	26
27	28	29	30			

July

S	M	T	W	T	F	S
				1	2	3
4	5	6	7	8	9	10
11	12	13	14	15	16	17
18	19	20	21	22	23	24
25	26	27	28	29	30	31

August

S	M	T	W	T	F	S
1	2	3	4	5	6	7
8	9	10	11	12	13	14
15	16	17	18	19	20	21
22	23	24	25	26	27	28
29	30	31				

September

S	M	T	W	T	F	S
			1	2	3	4
5	6	7	8	9	10	11
12	13	14	15	16	17	18
19	20	21	22	23	24	25
26	27	28	29	30		

October

S	M	T	W	T	F	S
					1	2
3	4	5	6	7	8	9
10	11	12	13	14	15	16
17	18	19	20	21	22	23
24	25	26	27	28	29	30
31						

November

S	M	T	W	T	F	S
	1	2	3	4	5	6
7	8	9	10	11	12	13
14	15	16	17	18	19	20
21	22	23	24	25	26	27
28	29	30				

December

S	M	T	W	T	F	S
			1	2	3	4
5	6	7	8	9	10	11
12	13	14	15	16	17	18
19	20	21	22	23	24	25
26	27	28	29	30	31	

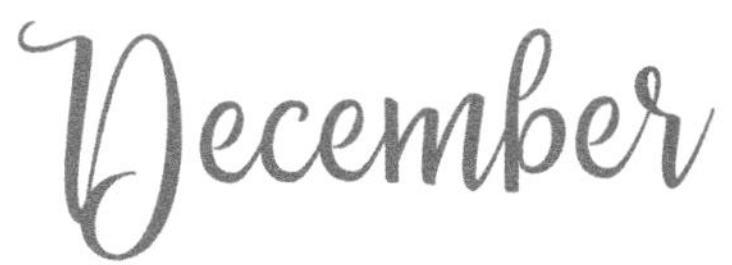

December 2020

SUNDAY	MONDAY	TUESDAY	WEDNESDAY
		1	2
6	7	8	9
13	14	15	16
20	21 First Day of Winter (Winter Solstice)	22	23
27	28	29	30

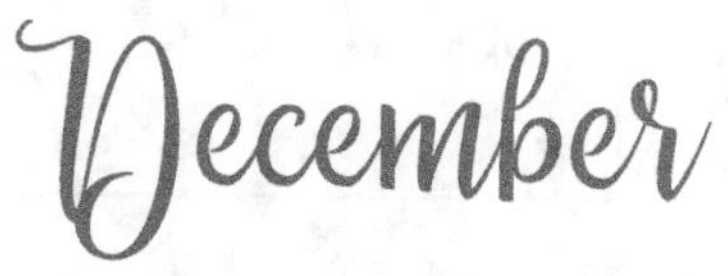

December

2020

THURSDAY	FRIDAY	SATURDAY	NOTES
3	4	5	○
			○
			○
			○
			○
10 Hanukkah Begins	11	12	○
			○
			○
			○
17	18 Hanukkah Ends	19	○
			○
			○
			○
			○
24 Christmas Eve	25 Christmas Day	26	○
			○
			○
			○
			○
31 New Year's Eve			NOTES

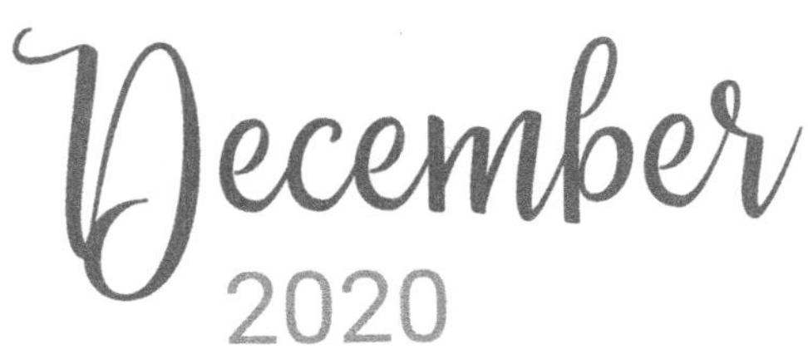

December
2020

December

S	M	T	W	T	F	S
		1	2	3	4	5
6	7	8	9	10	11	12
13	14	15	16	17	18	19
20	21	22	23	24	25	26
27	28	29	30	31		

30 MONDAY

01 TUESDAY

02 WEDNESDAY

03 THURSDAY

04 FRIDAY

05 SATURDAY

06 SUNDAY

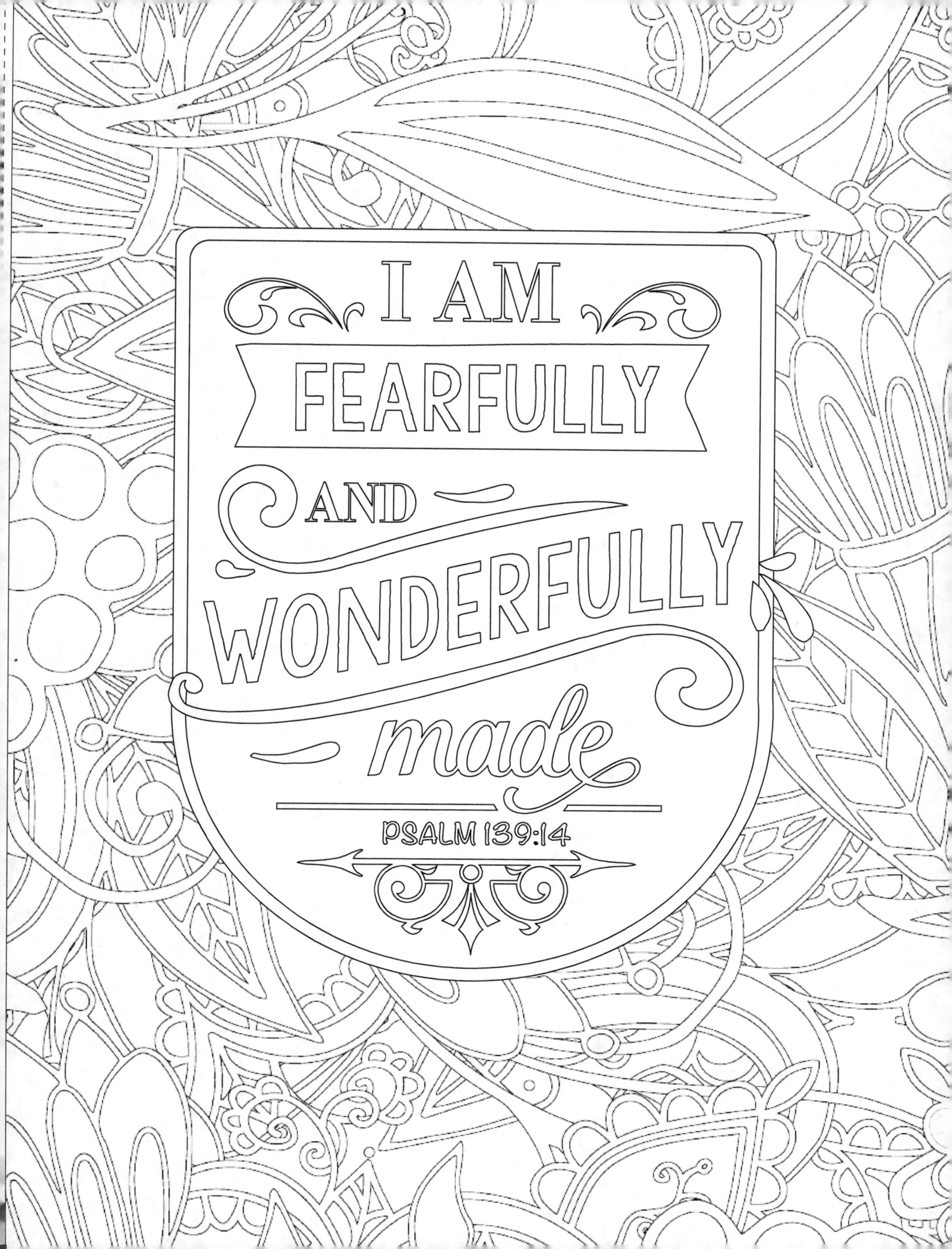

I AM
FEARFULLY
AND
WONDERFULLY
made
PSALM 139:14

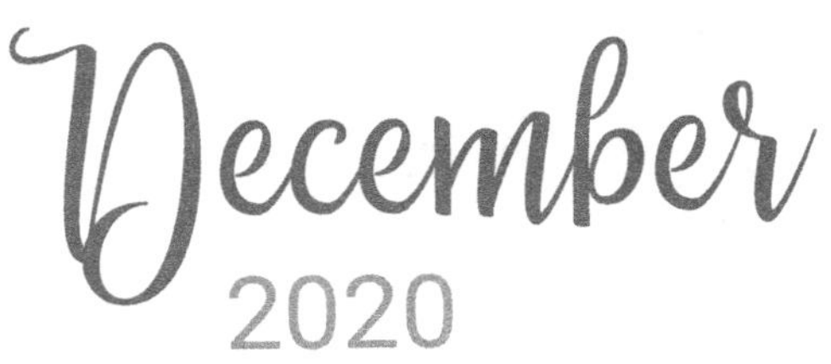

December
2020

07 MONDAY

08 TUESDAY

09 WEDNESDAY

10 THURSDAY Hanukkah Begins

11 FRIDAY

12 SATURDAY

13 SUNDAY

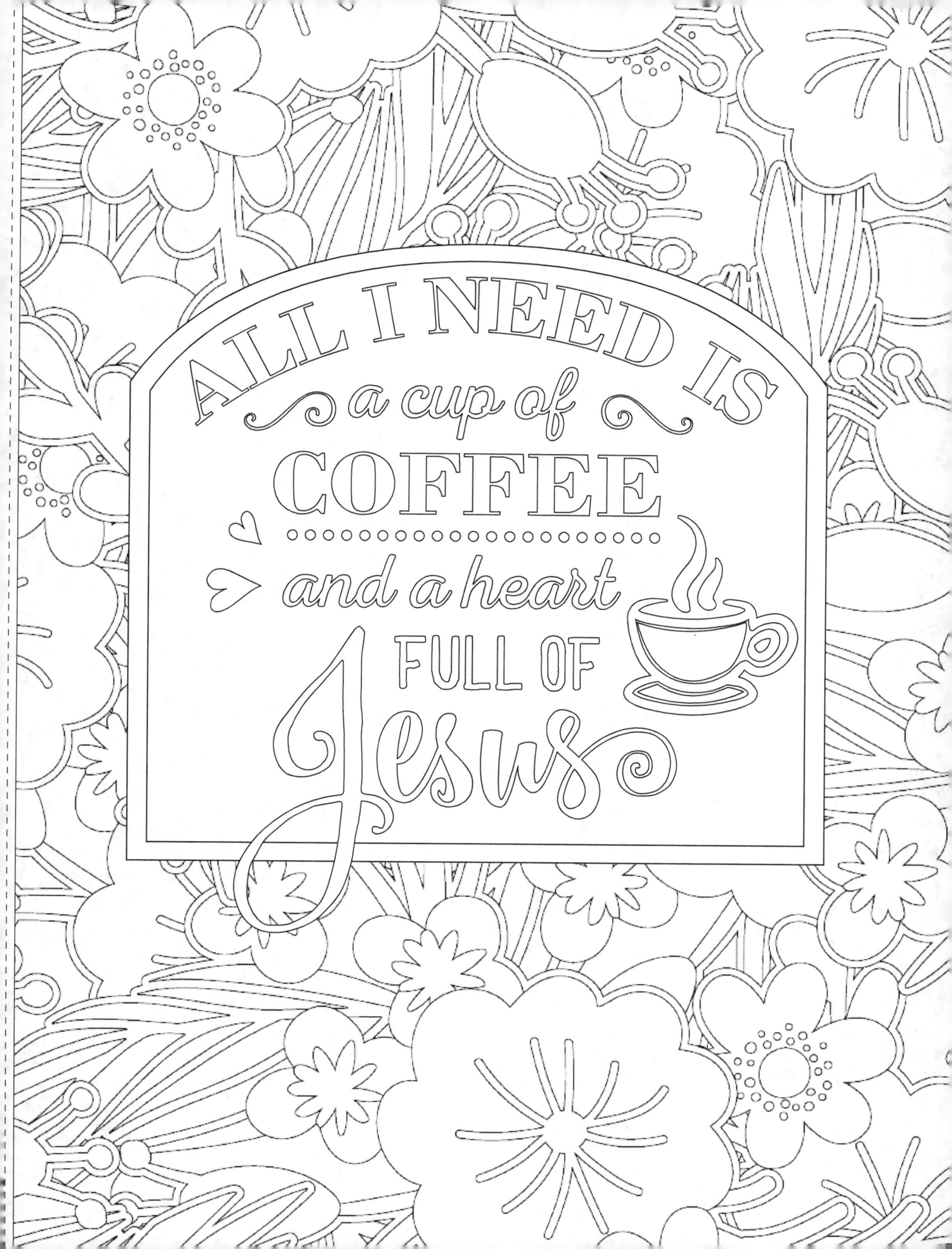

ALL I NEED IS
a cup of
COFFEE
and a heart
FULL OF
Jesus

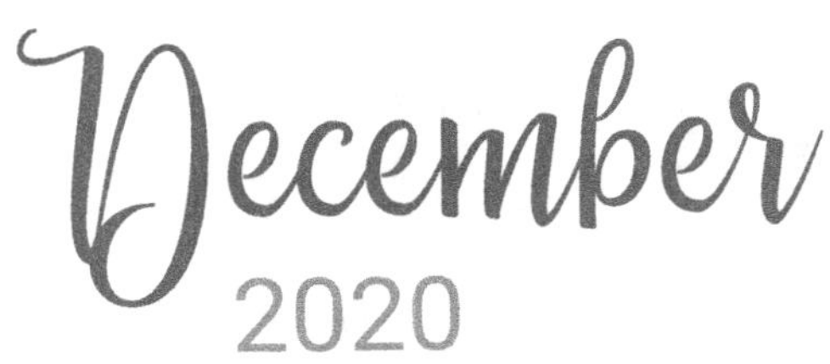

December
2020

14 MONDAY

15 TUESDAY

16 WEDNESDAY

17 THURSDAY

18 FRIDAY   Hanukkah Ends

19 SATURDAY

20 SUNDAY

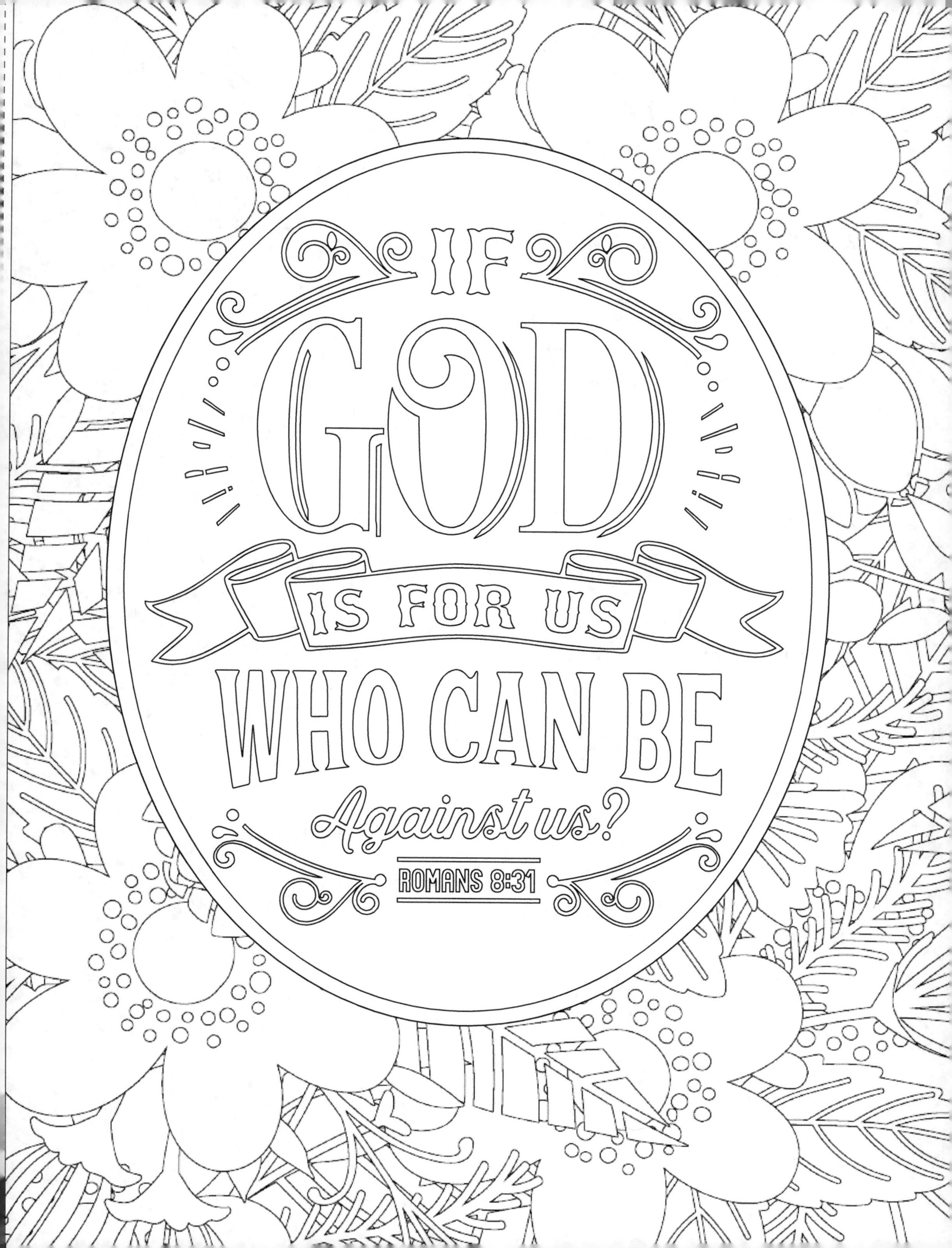

IF
GOD
IS FOR US
WHO CAN BE
Against us?
ROMANS 8:31

December
2020

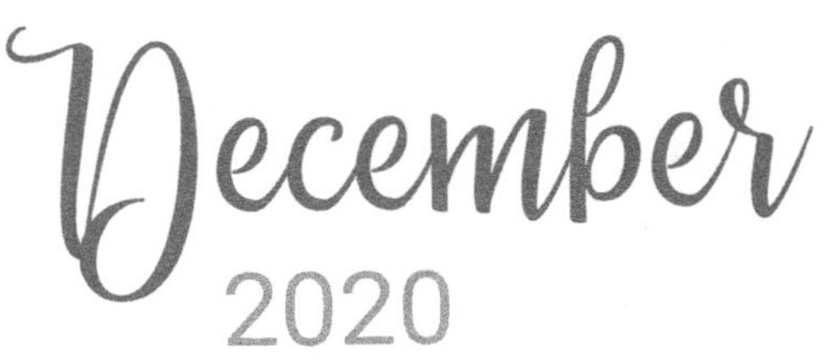

21 MONDAY First Day of Winter (Winter Solstice)

22 TUESDAY

23 WEDNESDAY

24 THURSDAY Christmas Eve

25 FRIDAY Christmas Day

26 SATURDAY

27 SUNDAY

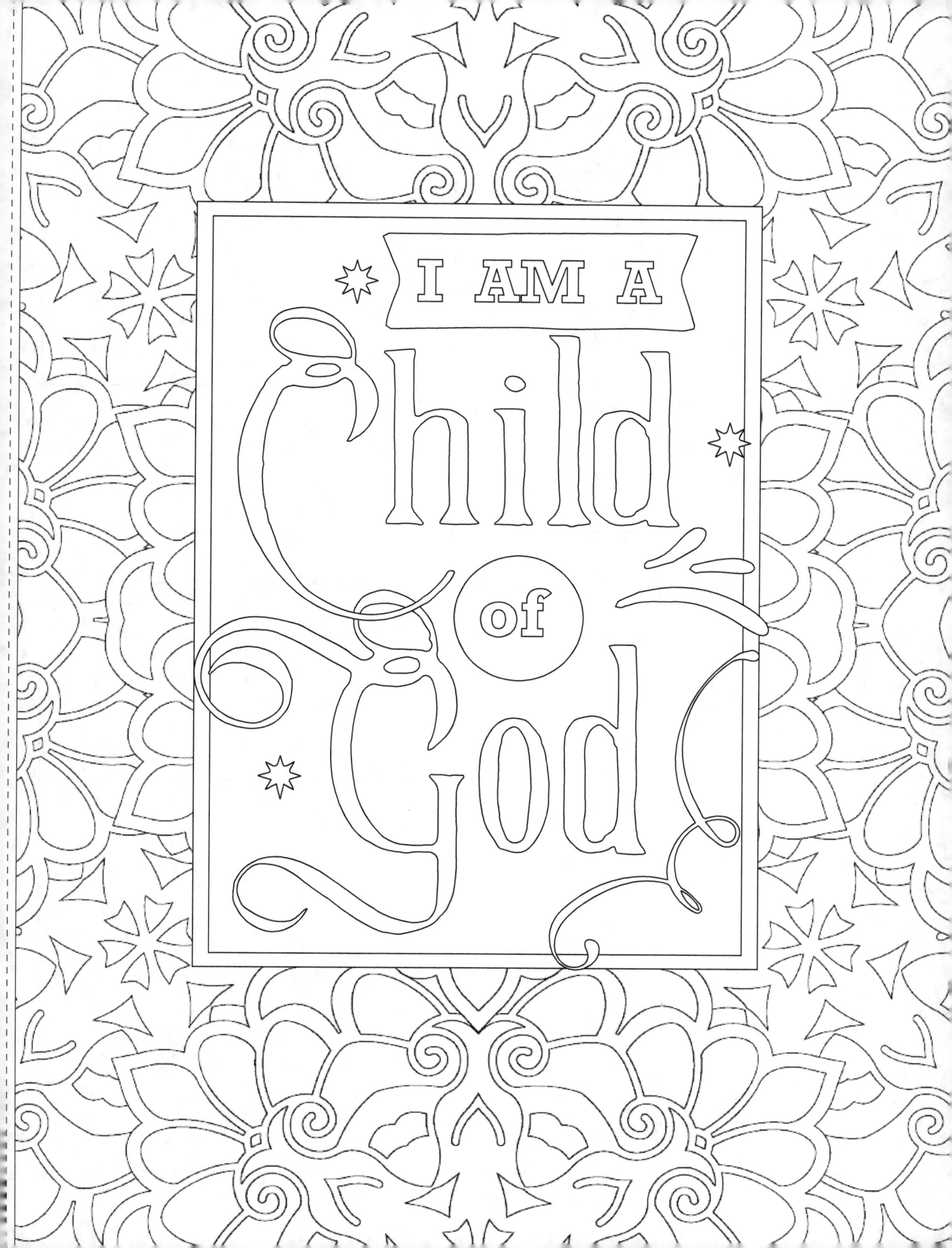

I AM A
Child
of
God

January 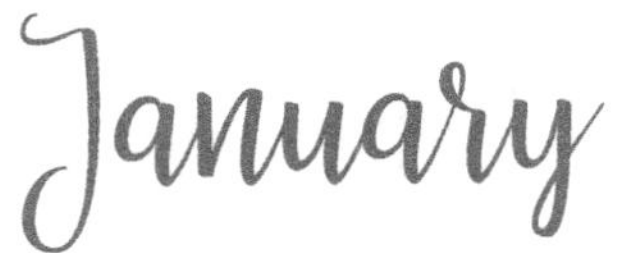 2021

SUNDAY	MONDAY	TUESDAY	WEDNESDAY
3	4	5	6
10	11	12	13
17	18 Martin Luther King Jr. Day	19	20
24 31	25	26	27

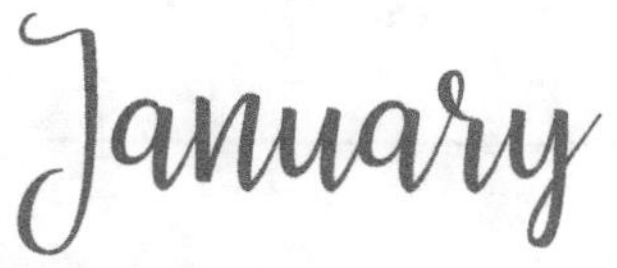

January 2021

THURSDAY	FRIDAY	SATURDAY	NOTES
	1 New Year's Day	2	○
			○
			○
			○
			○
7	8	9	○
			○
			○
			○
14	15	16	○
			○
			○
			○
			○
21	22	23	○
			○
			○
			○
			○
28	29	30	NOTES

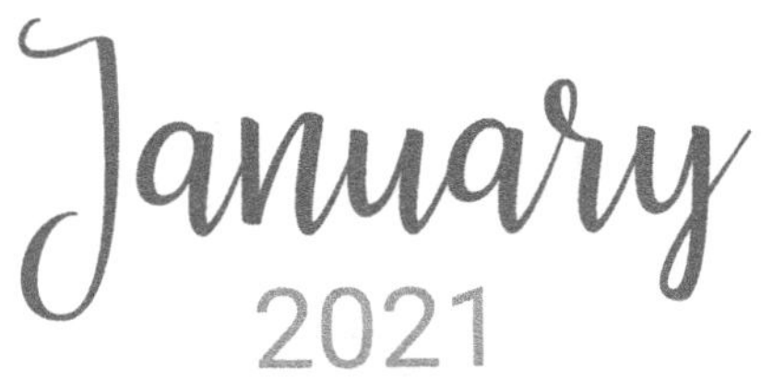

January
2021

28 MONDAY

29 TUESDAY

30 WEDNESDAY

31 THURSDAY New Year's Eve

01 FRIDAY New Year's Day

02 SATURDAY

03 SUNDAY

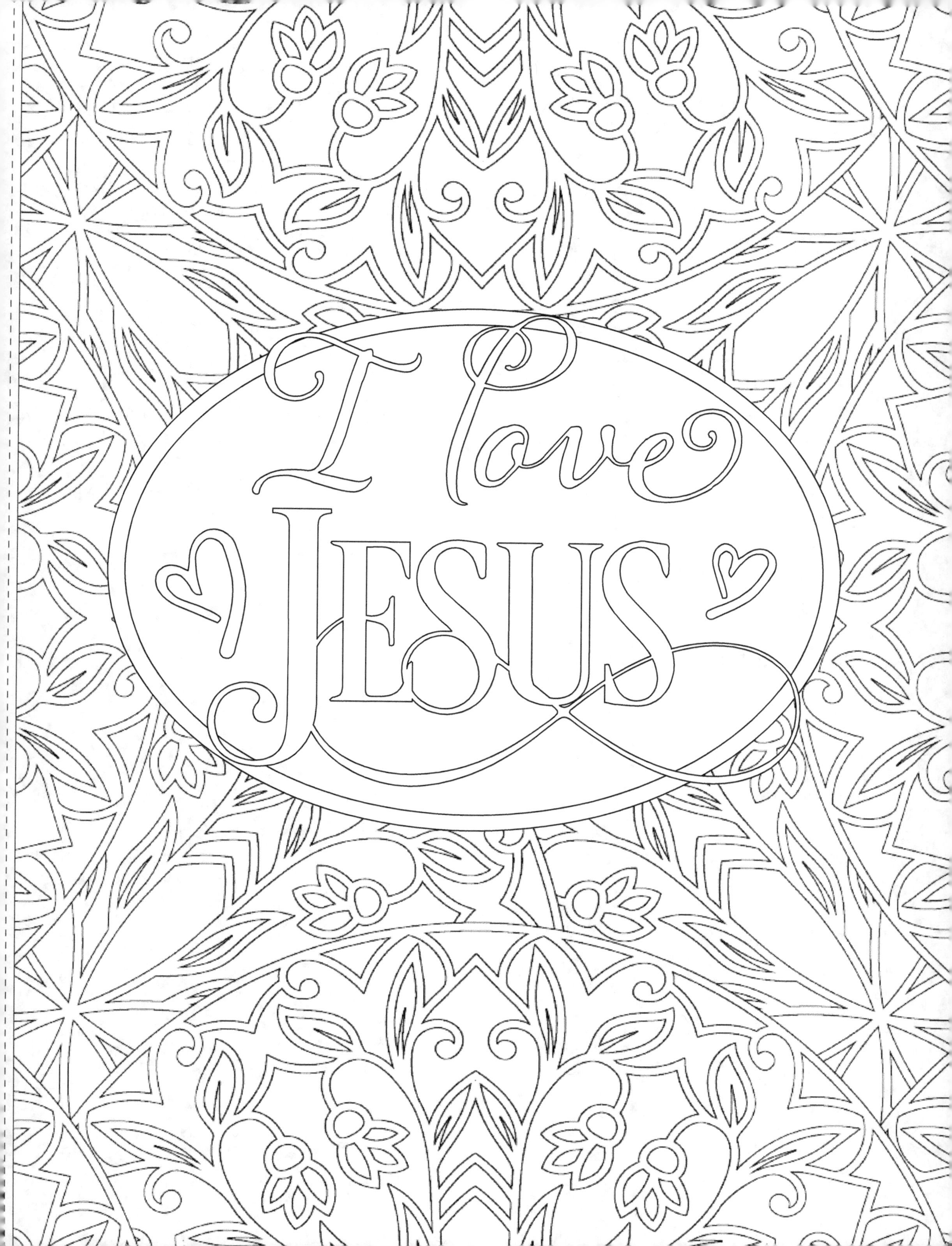

I Love
JESUS

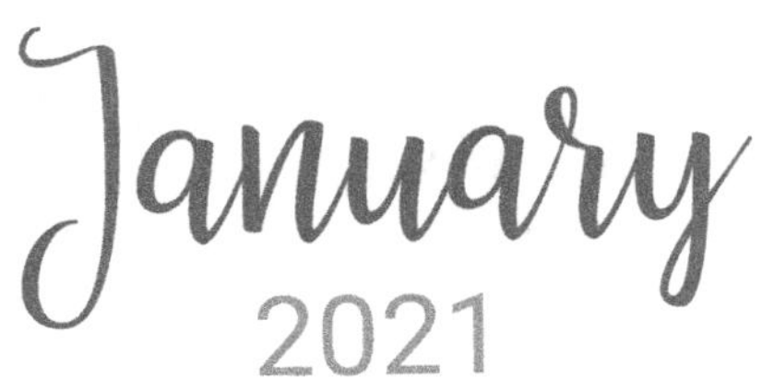

January
2021

04 MONDAY

05 TUESDAY

06 WEDNESDAY

07 THURSDAY

08 FRIDAY

09 SATURDAY

10 SUNDAY

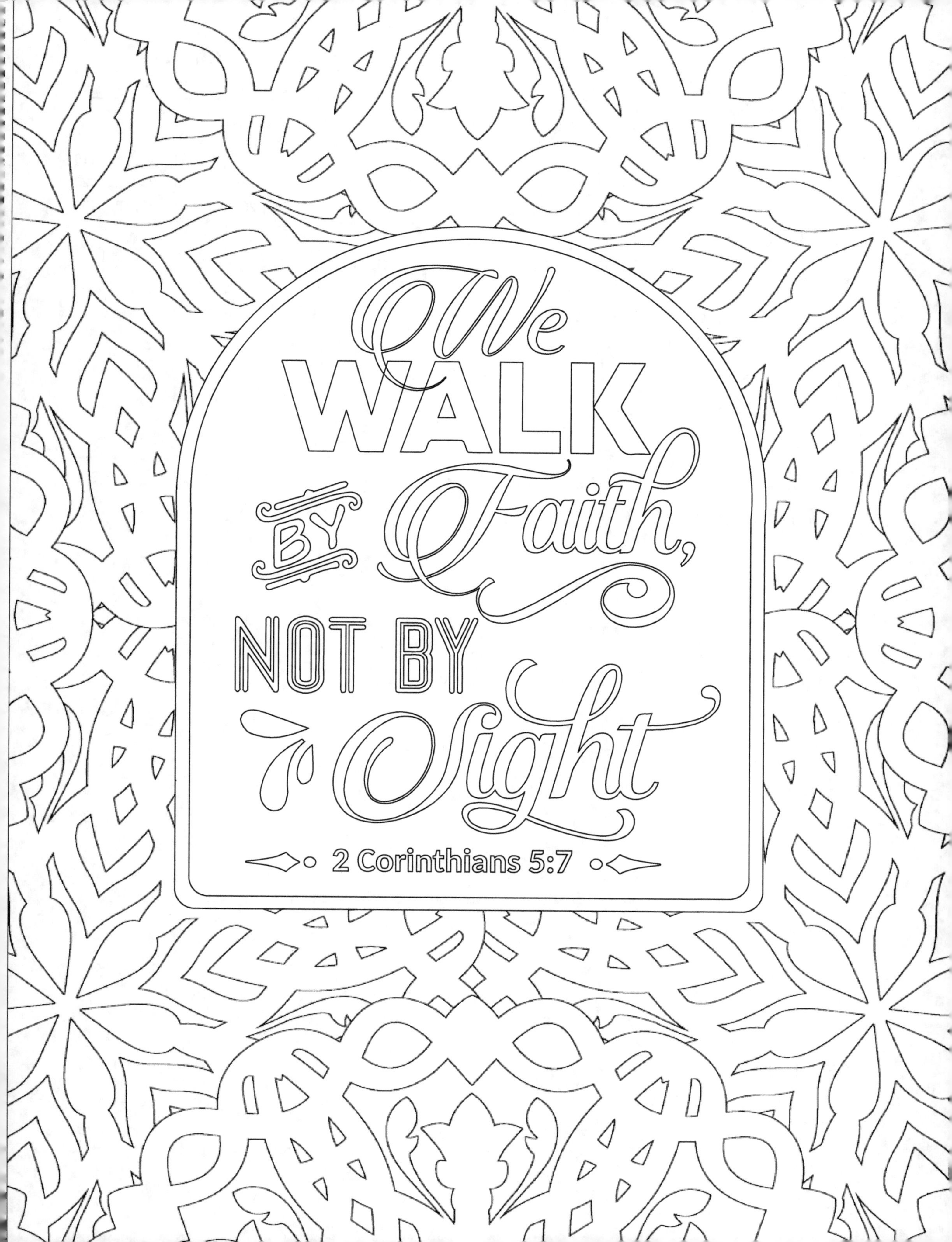

We
WALK
BY Faith,
NOT BY Sight
2 Corinthians 5:7

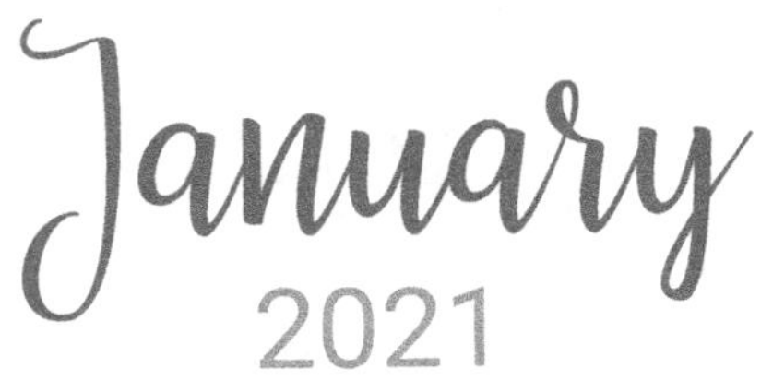

January
2021

11 MONDAY

12 TUESDAY

13 WEDNESDAY

14 THURSDAY

15 FRIDAY

16 SATURDAY

17 SUNDAY

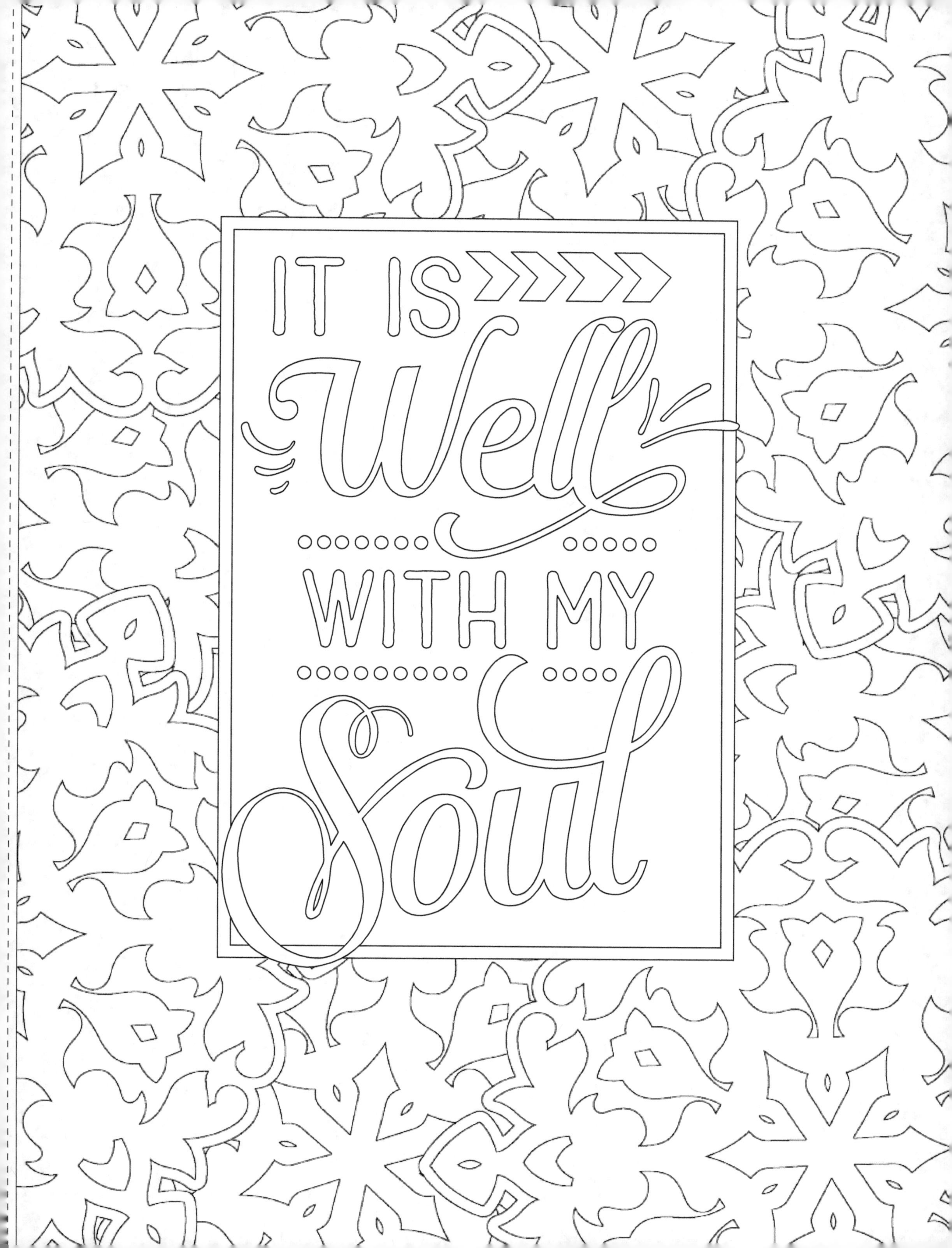

IT IS
Well
WITH MY
Soul

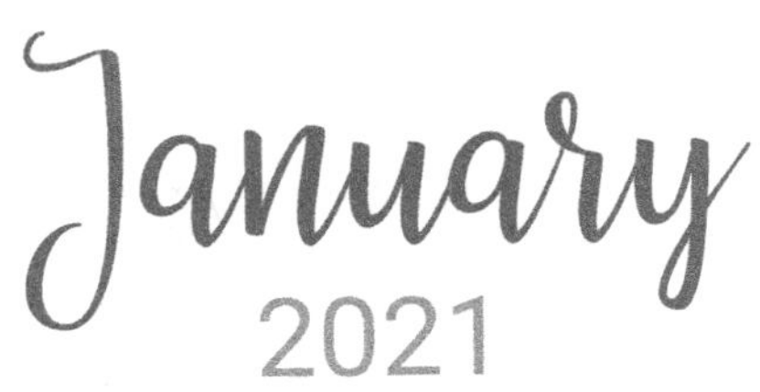

January
2021

18 MONDAY   Martin Luther King Jr. Day

19 TUESDAY

20 WEDNESDAY

21 THURSDAY

22 FRIDAY

23 SATURDAY

24 SUNDAY

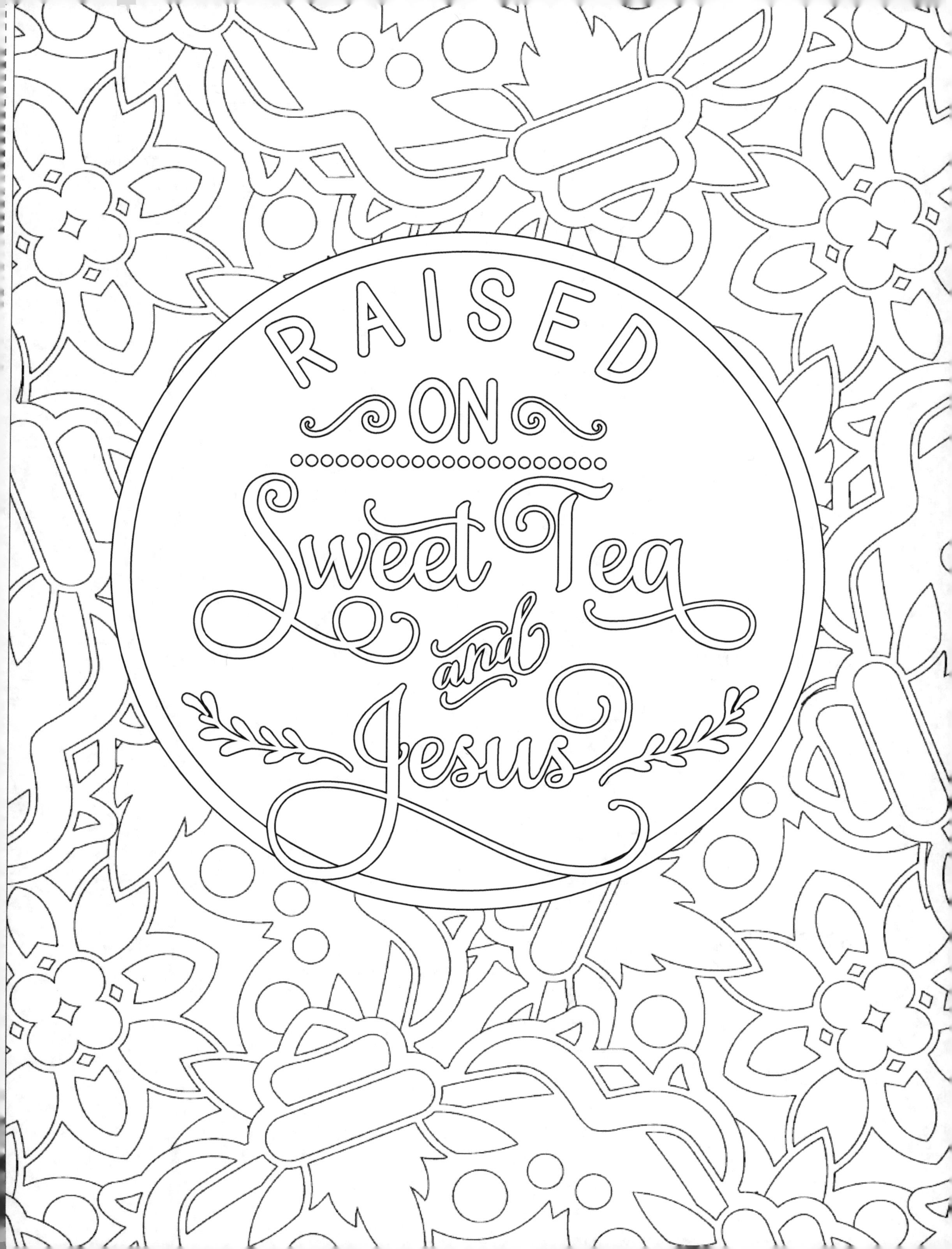
RAISED
ON
Sweet Tea
and
Jesus

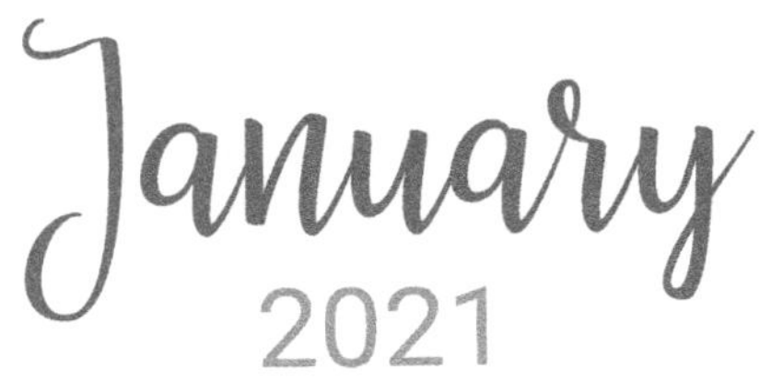

January
2021

25 MONDAY

26 TUESDAY

27 WEDNESDAY

28 THURSDAY

29 FRIDAY

30 SATURDAY

31 SUNDAY

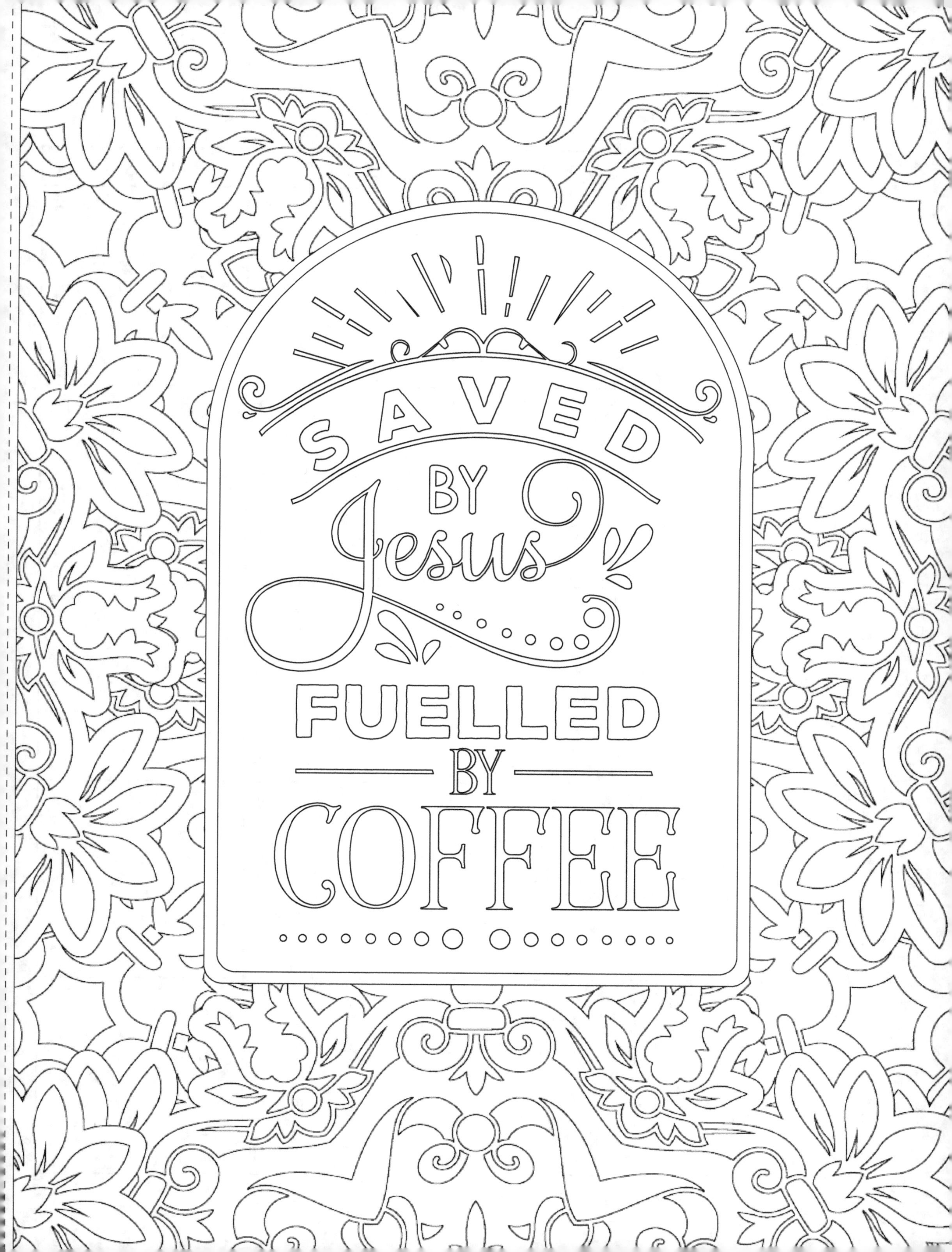

SAVED
BY
Jesus
FUELLED
BY
COFFEE

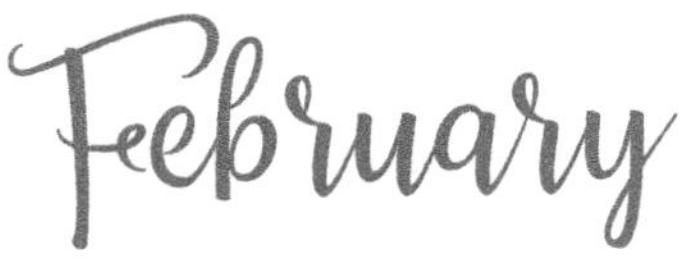

February 2021

SUNDAY	MONDAY	TUESDAY	WEDNESDAY
	1	2	3
7	8	9	10
14 Valentine's Day	15 President's Day	16	17
21	22	23	24
28			

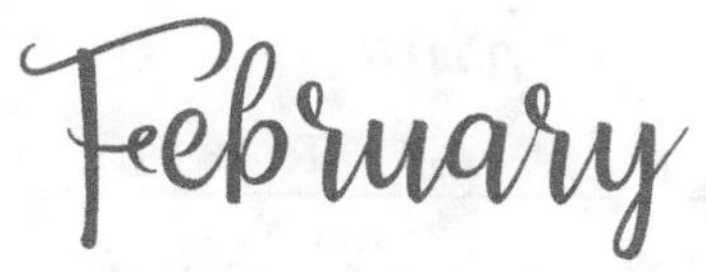

February

2021

THURSDAY	FRIDAY	SATURDAY	NOTES
4	5	6	○
			○
			○
			○
			○
11	12	13	○
			○
			○
			○
18	19	20	○
			○
			○
			○
			○
25	26	27	○
			○
			○
			○
			○
			NOTES

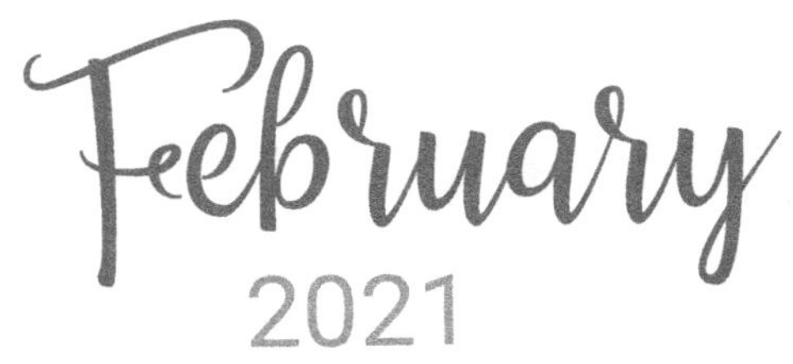

February
2021

01 MONDAY

02 TUESDAY

03 WEDNESDAY

04 THURSDAY

05 FRIDAY

06 SATURDAY

07 SUNDAY

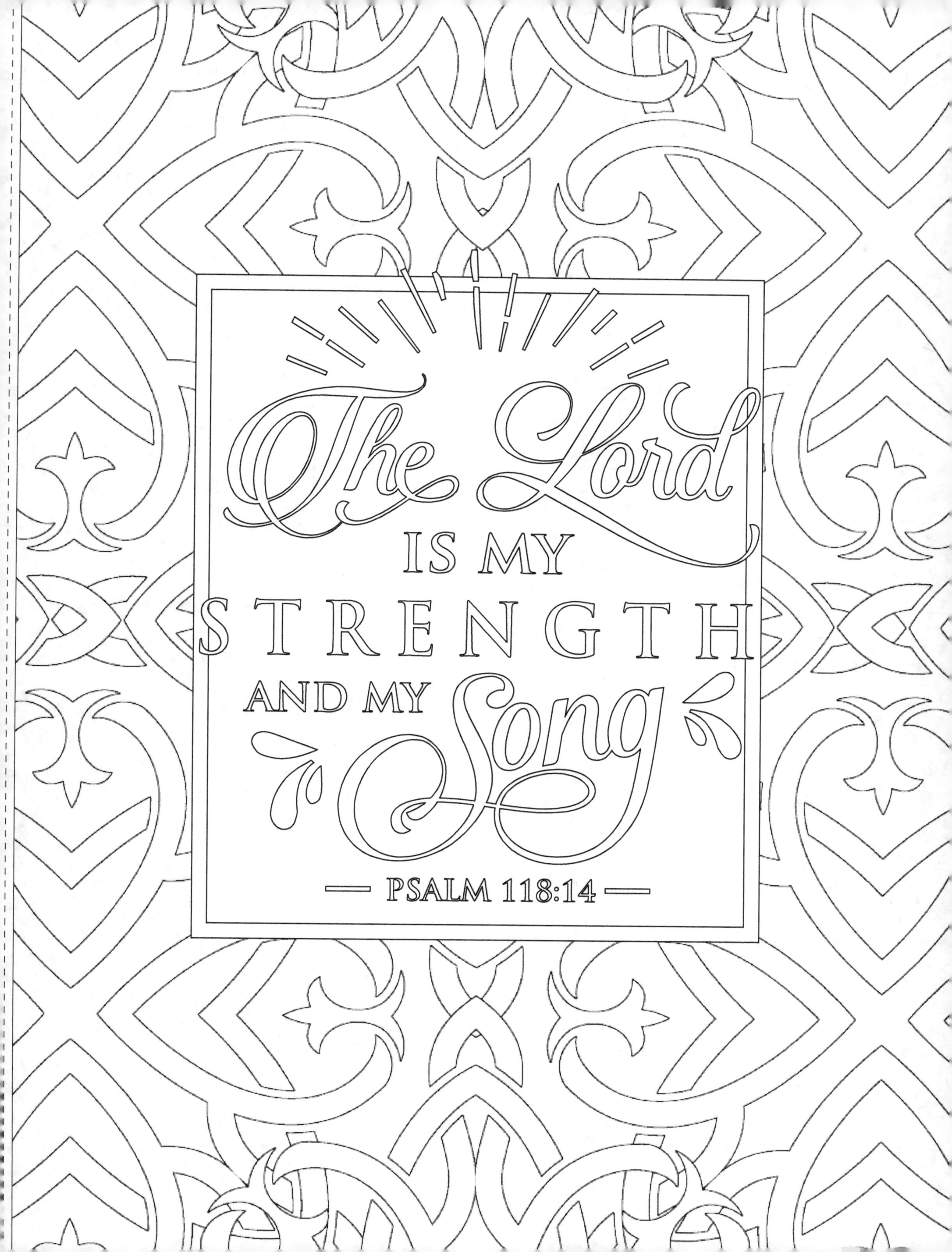

The Lord
IS MY
STRENGTH
AND MY Song
— PSALM 118:14 —

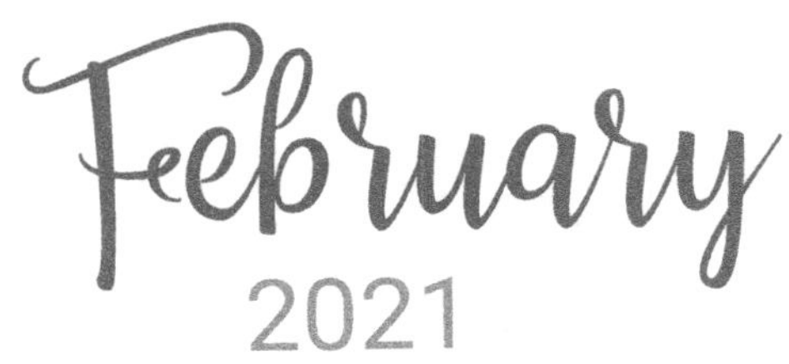

February
2021

08 MONDAY

09 TUESDAY

10 WEDNESDAY

11 THURSDAY

12 FRIDAY

13 SATURDAY

14 SUNDAY   Valentine's Day

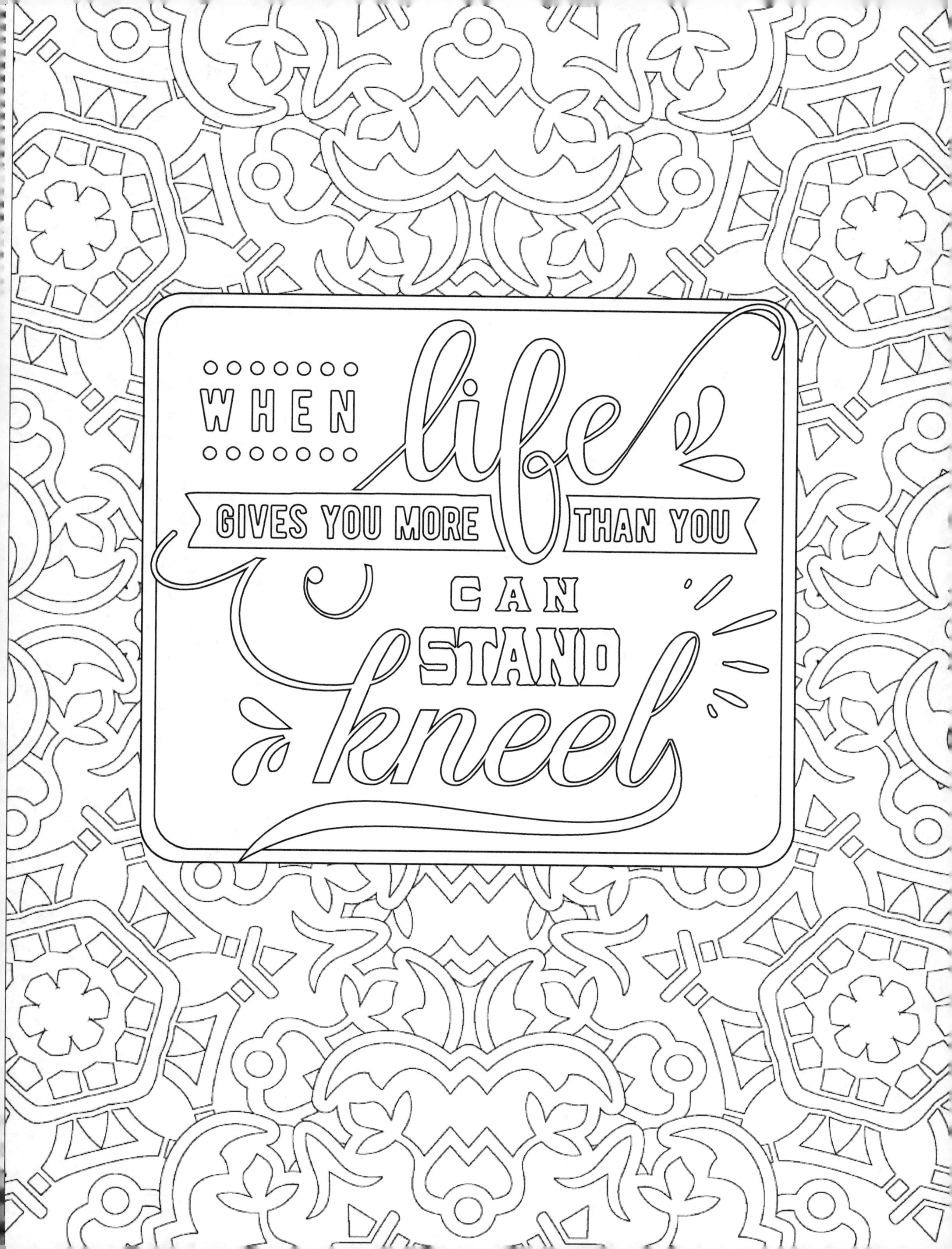

WHEN life
GIVES YOU MORE THAN YOU
CAN
STAND
kneel

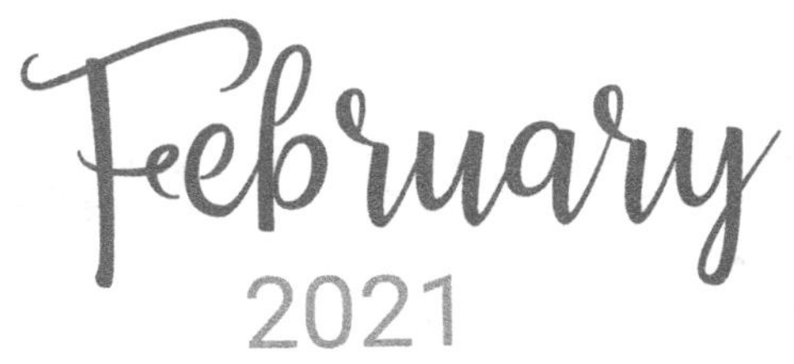

February
2021

15 MONDAY · President's Day

16 TUESDAY

17 WEDNESDAY

18 THURSDAY

19 FRIDAY

20 SATURDAY

21 SUNDAY

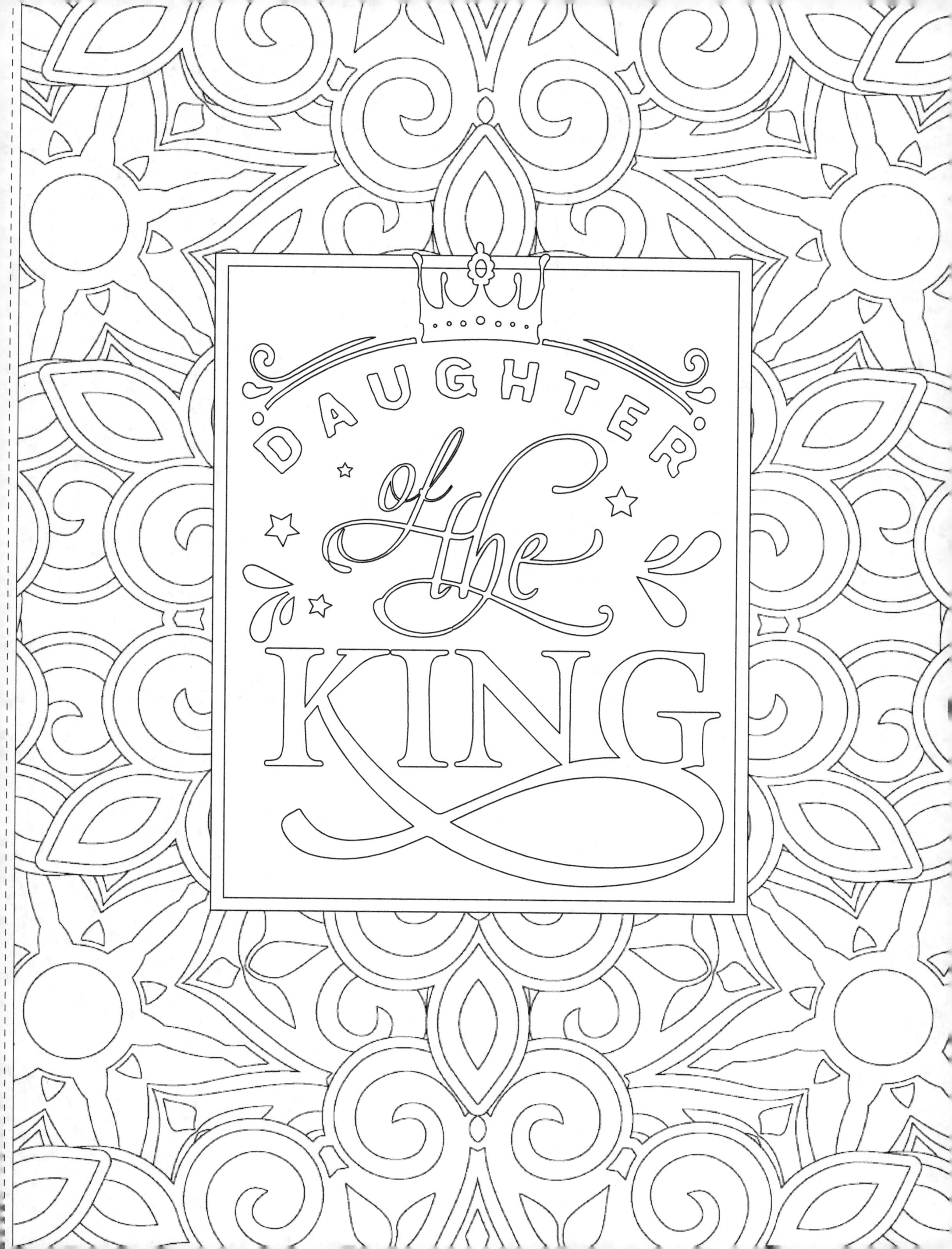
DAUGHTER
of the
KING

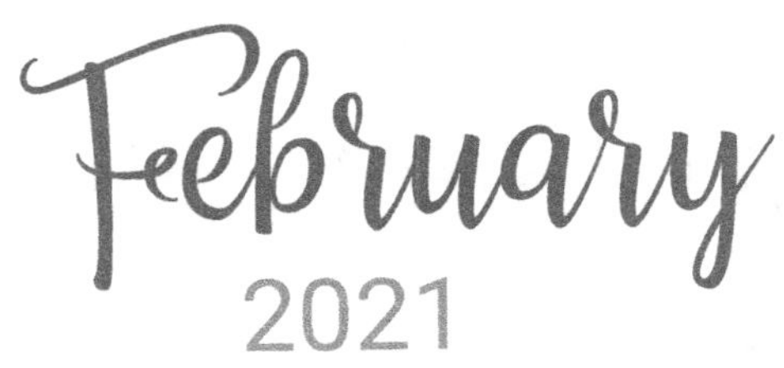

February
2021

22 MONDAY

23 TUESDAY

24 WEDNESDAY

25 THURSDAY

26 FRIDAY

27 SATURDAY

28 SUNDAY

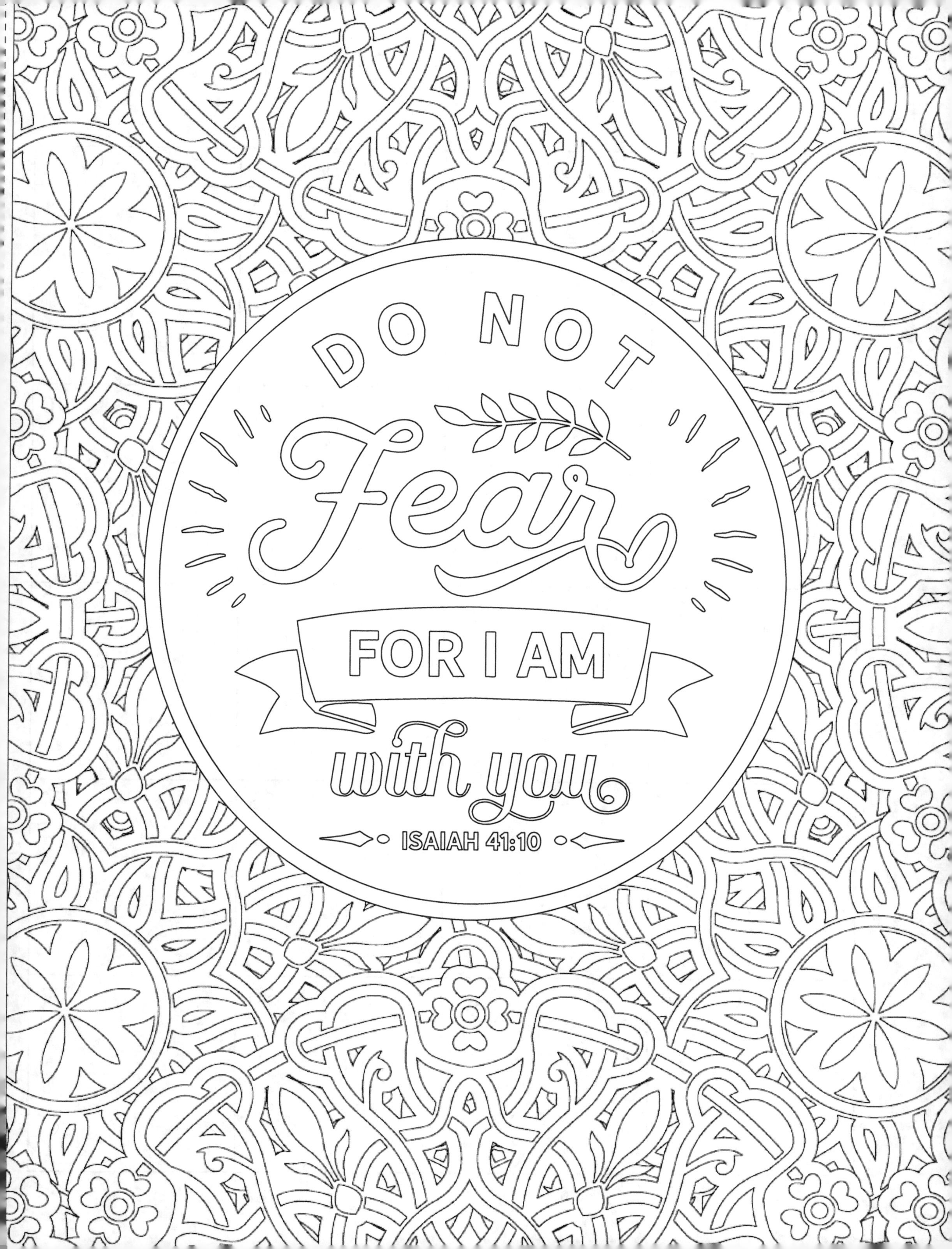

DO NOT
Fear
FOR I AM
with you
ISAIAH 41:10

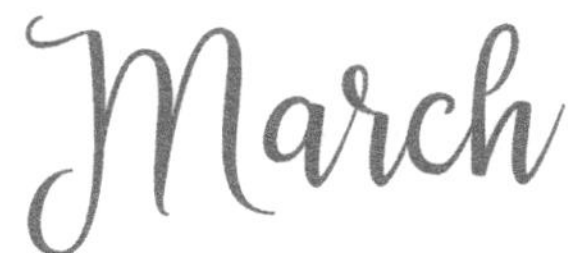

March

2021

SUNDAY	MONDAY	TUESDAY	WEDNESDAY
	1	2	3
7	8	9	10
14 Daylight Savings Time Begins	15	16	17
21	22	23	24
28	29	30	31

THURSDAY	FRIDAY	SATURDAY	NOTES
4	5	6	○
			○
			○
			○
			○
11	12	13	○
			○
			○
			○
18	19	20 First Day of Spring	○
			○
			○
			○
25	26	27 Passover Begins	○
			○
			○
			○
			○
			NOTES

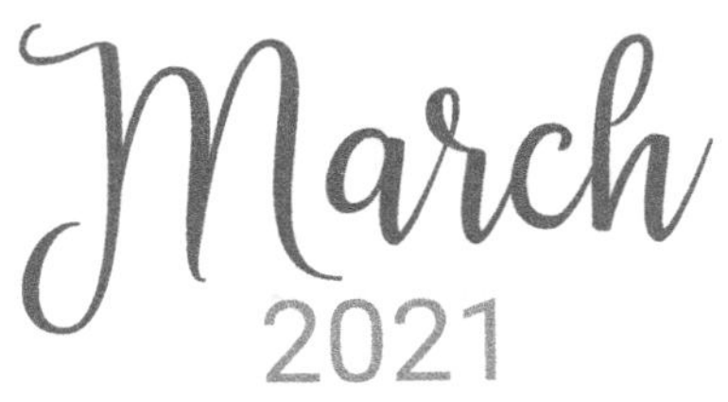

March
2021

01 MONDAY

02 TUESDAY

03 WEDNESDAY

04 THURSDAY

05 FRIDAY

06 SATURDAY

07 SUNDAY

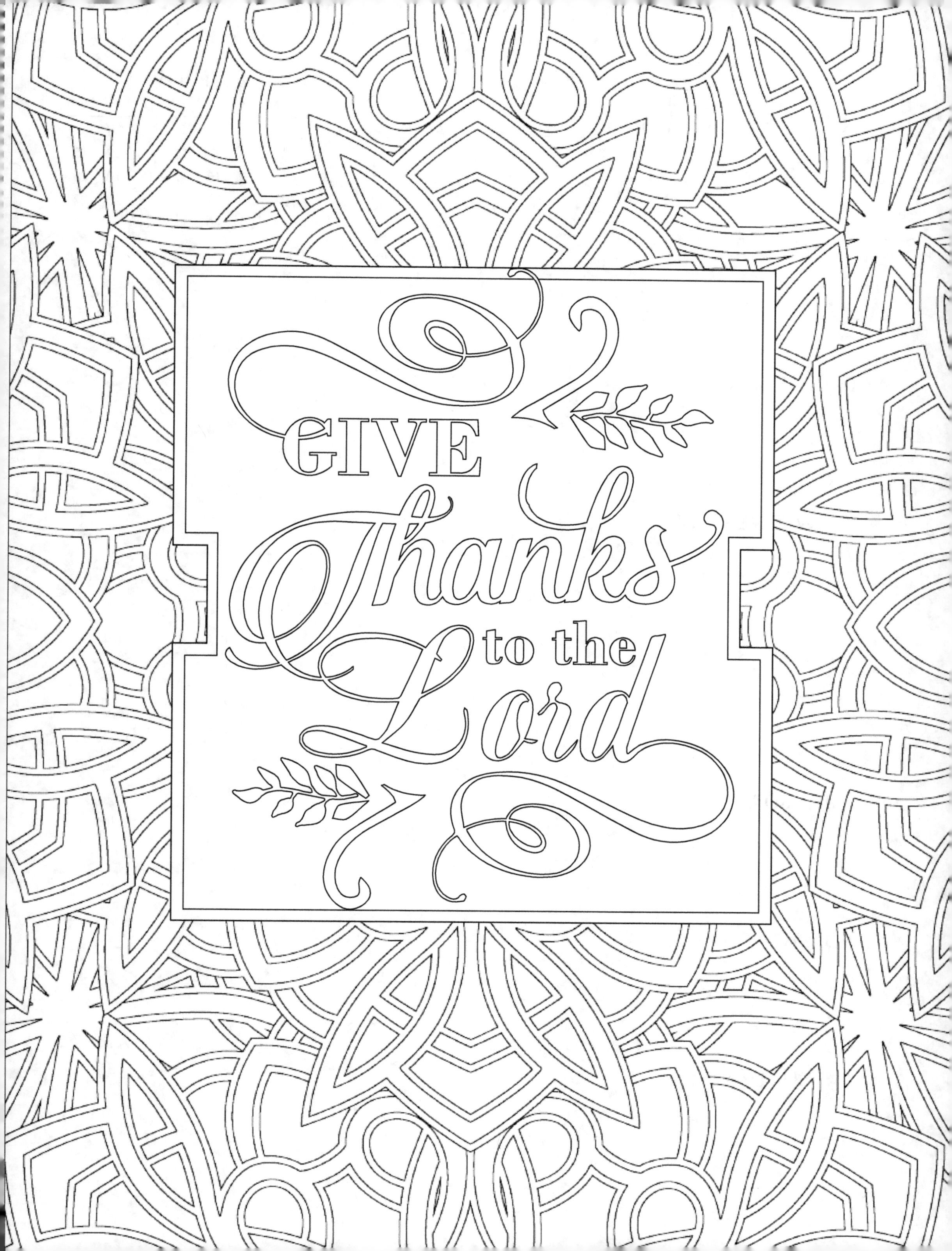
GIVE
Thanks
to the
Lord

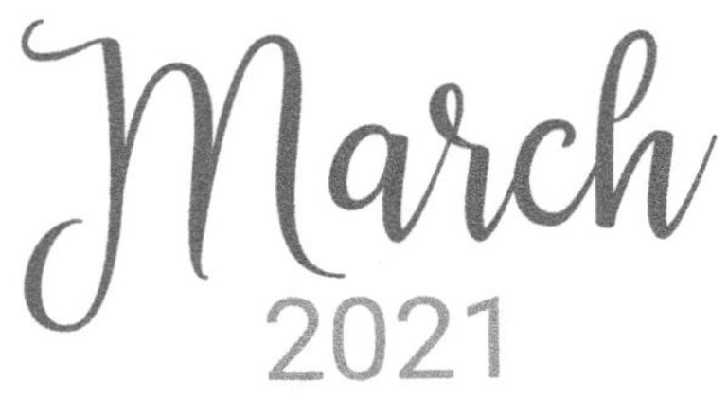

March
2021

08 MONDAY

09 TUESDAY

10 WEDNESDAY

11 THURSDAY

12 FRIDAY

13 SATURDAY

14 SUNDAY   Daylight Savings Time Begins

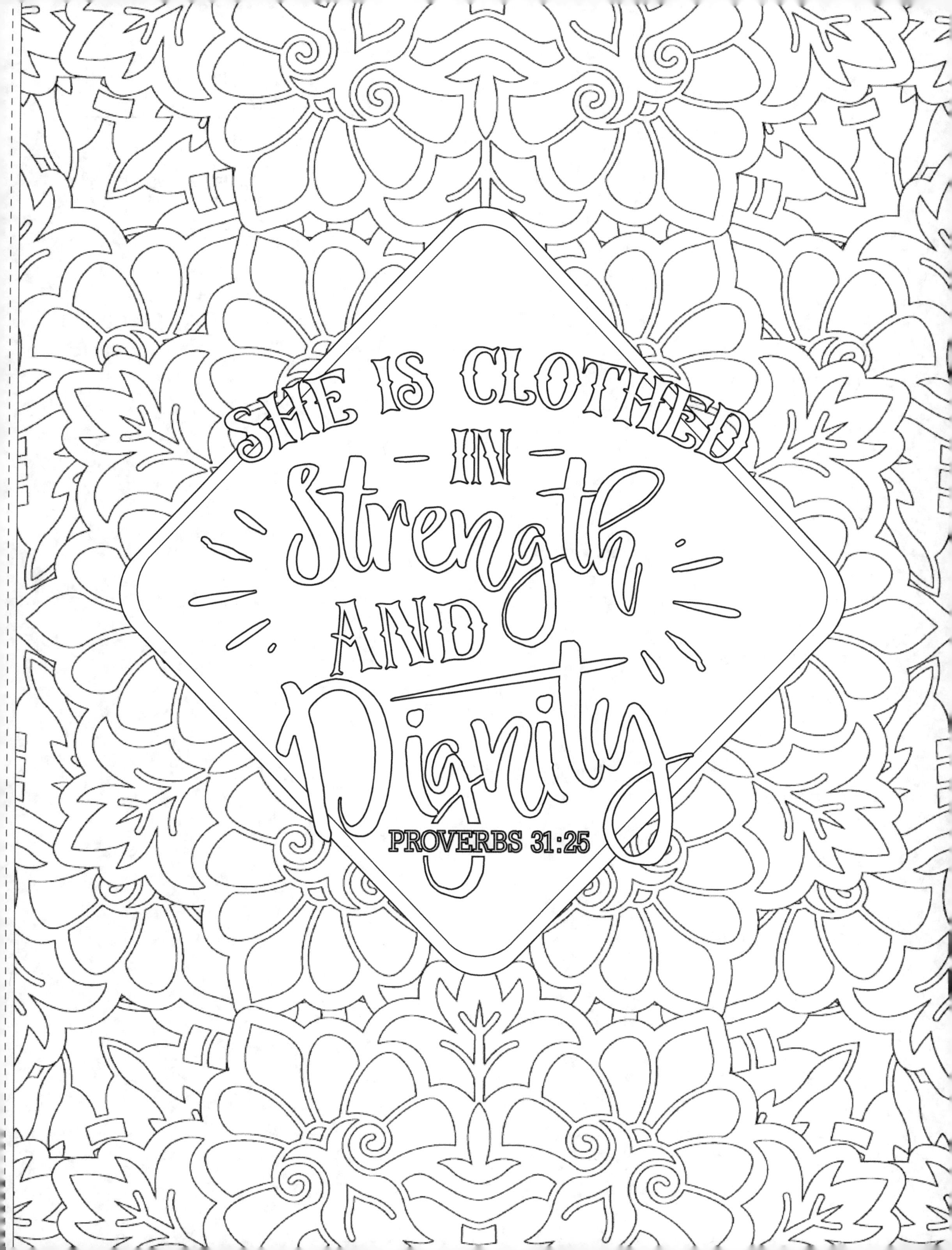

SHE IS CLOTHED
IN
Strength
AND
Dignity
PROVERBS 31:25

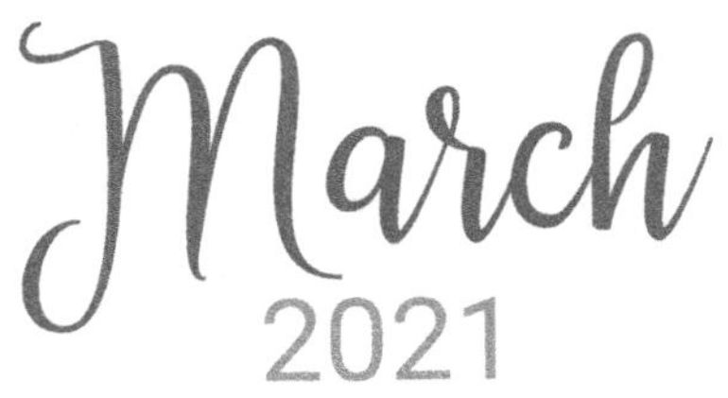

March
2021

15 MONDAY

16 TUESDAY

17 WEDNESDAY　St. Patrick's Day

18 THURSDAY

19 FRIDAY

20 SATURDAY　First Day of Spring

21 SUNDAY

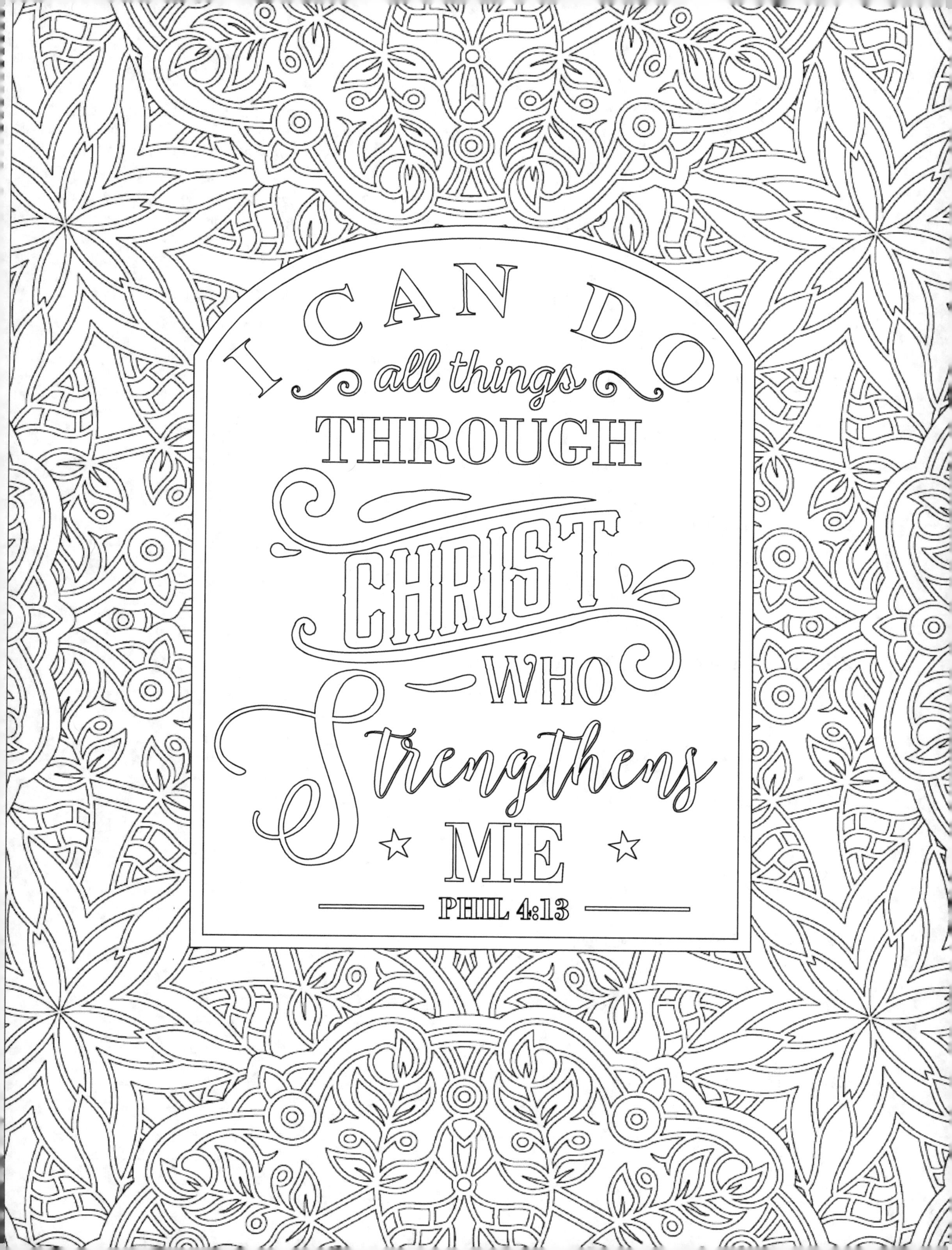

I CAN DO
all things
THROUGH
CHRIST
WHO
Strengthens
ME
PHIL 4:13

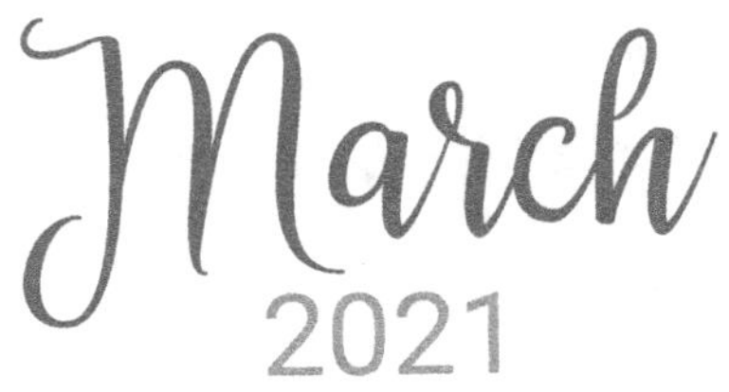

March
2021

22 MONDAY

23 TUESDAY

24 WEDNESDAY

25 THURSDAY

26 FRIDAY

27 SATURDAY   Passover Begins

28 SUNDAY

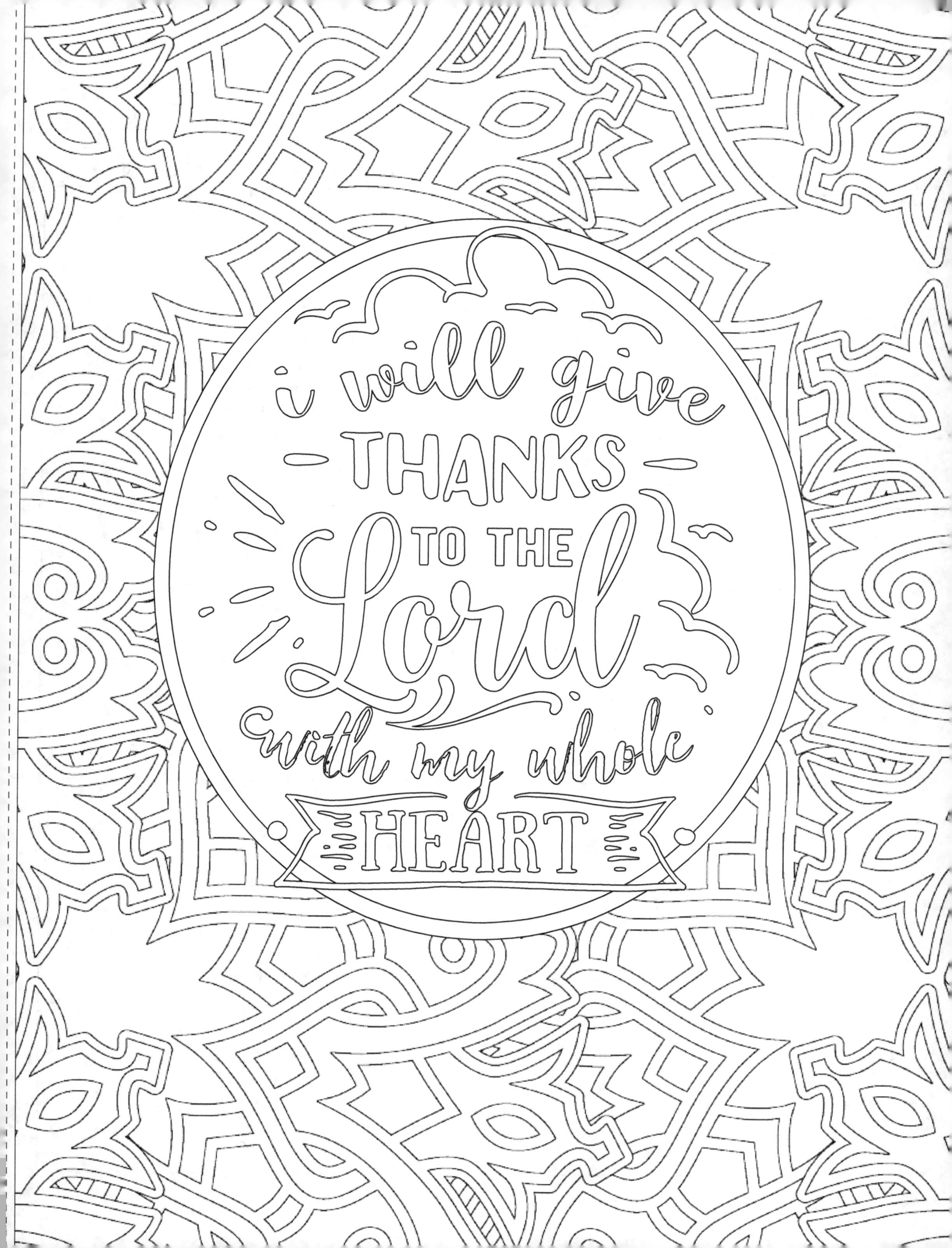

i will give
THANKS
TO THE
Lord
with my whole
HEART

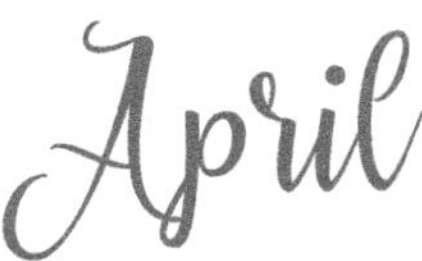

April

2021

SUNDAY	MONDAY	TUESDAY	WEDNESDAY
4 Easter (Passover Ends)	5	6	7
11	12	13	14
18	19	20	21
25	26	27	28

April

2021

THURSDAY	FRIDAY	SATURDAY	NOTES
1	2 Good Friday	3	○
			○
			○
			○
			○
8	9	10	○
			○
			○
			○
			○
15 Tax Day	16	17	○
			○
			○
			○
22 Earth Day	23	24	○
			○
			○
			○
			○
29	30		NOTES

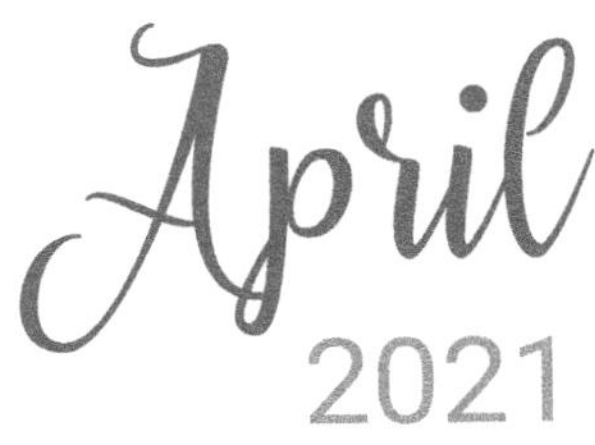

April
2021

29 MONDAY

30 TUESDAY

31 WEDNESDAY

01 THURSDAY

02 FRIDAY Good Friday

03 SATURDAY

04 SUNDAY Easter (Passover Ends)

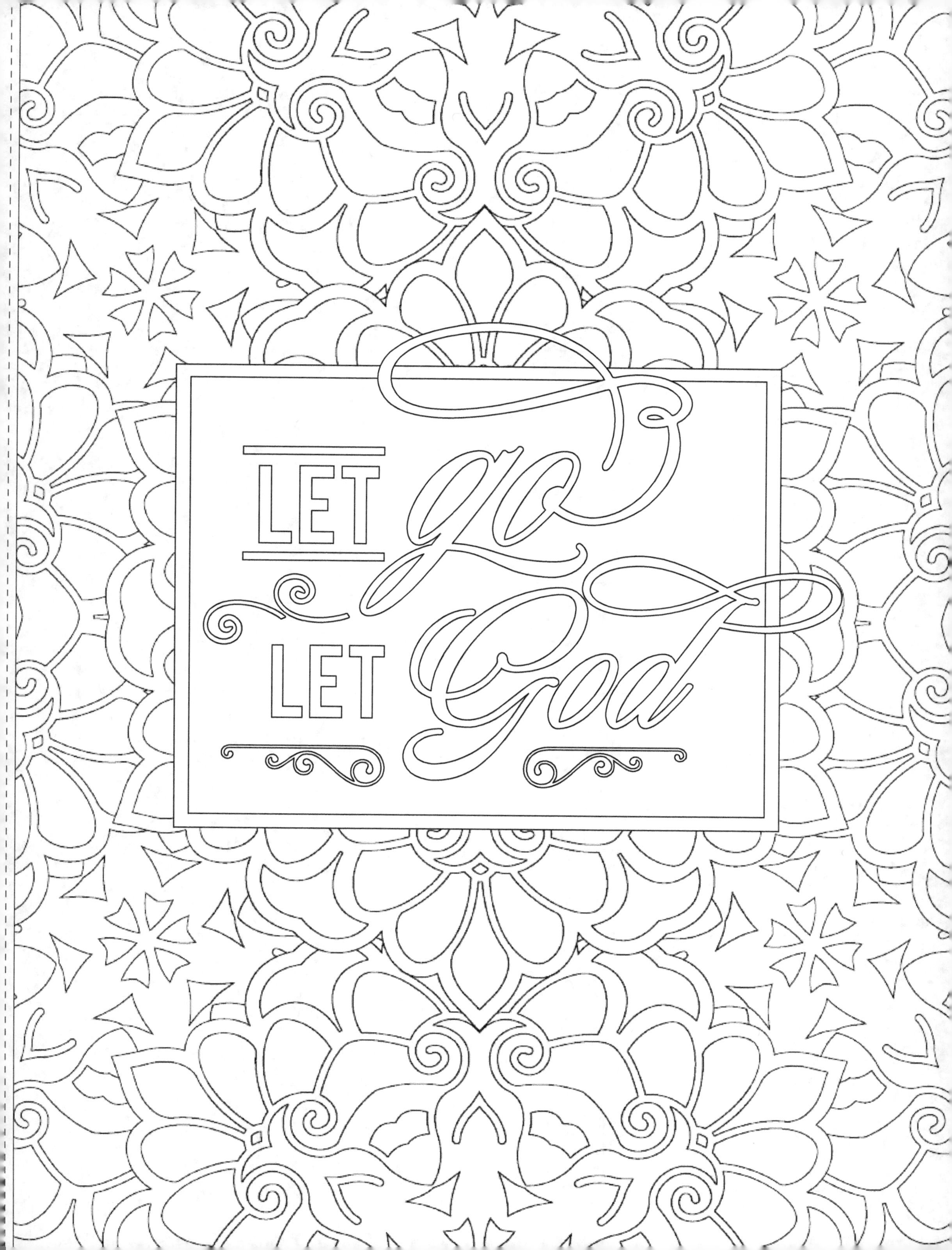

LET go
LET God

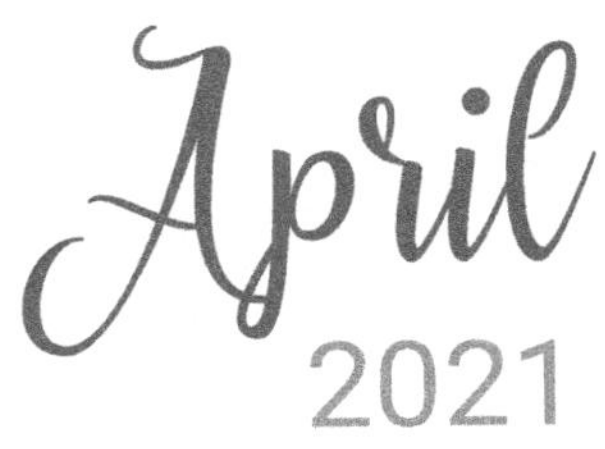

April
2021

05 MONDAY

06 TUESDAY

07 WEDNESDAY

08 THURSDAY

09 FRIDAY

10 SATURDAY

11 SUNDAY

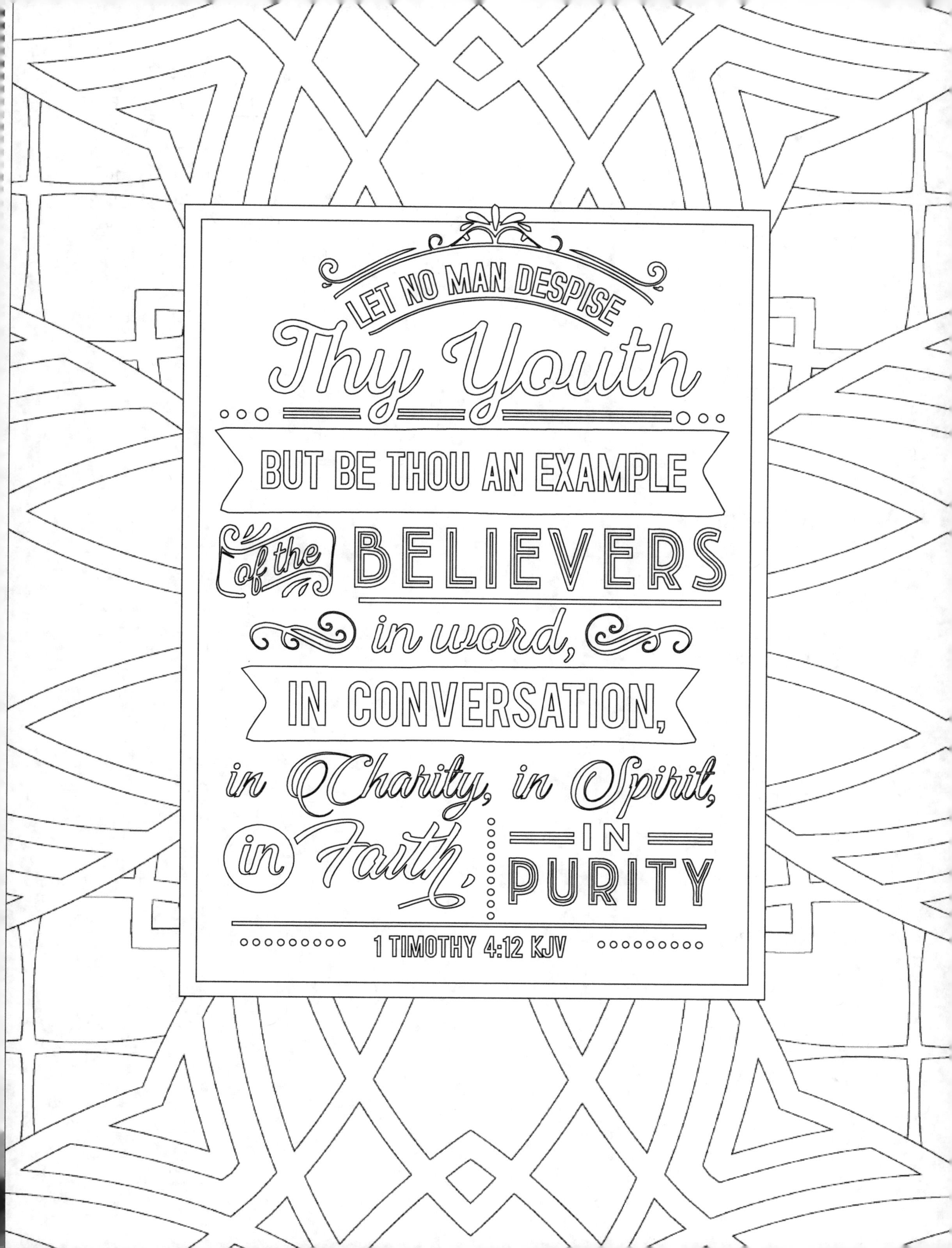

LET NO MAN DESPISE
Thy Youth
BUT BE THOU AN EXAMPLE
of the BELIEVERS
in word,
IN CONVERSATION,
in Charity, in Spirit,
in Faith, IN PURITY
1 TIMOTHY 4:12 KJV

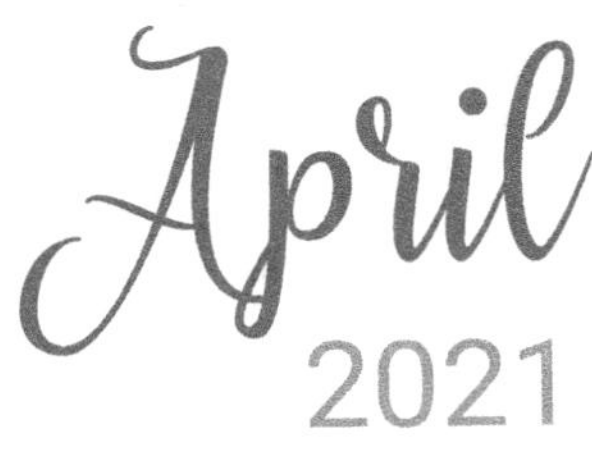

April
2021

12 MONDAY

13 TUESDAY

14 WEDNESDAY

15 THURSDAY Tax Day

16 FRIDAY

17 SATURDAY

18 SUNDAY

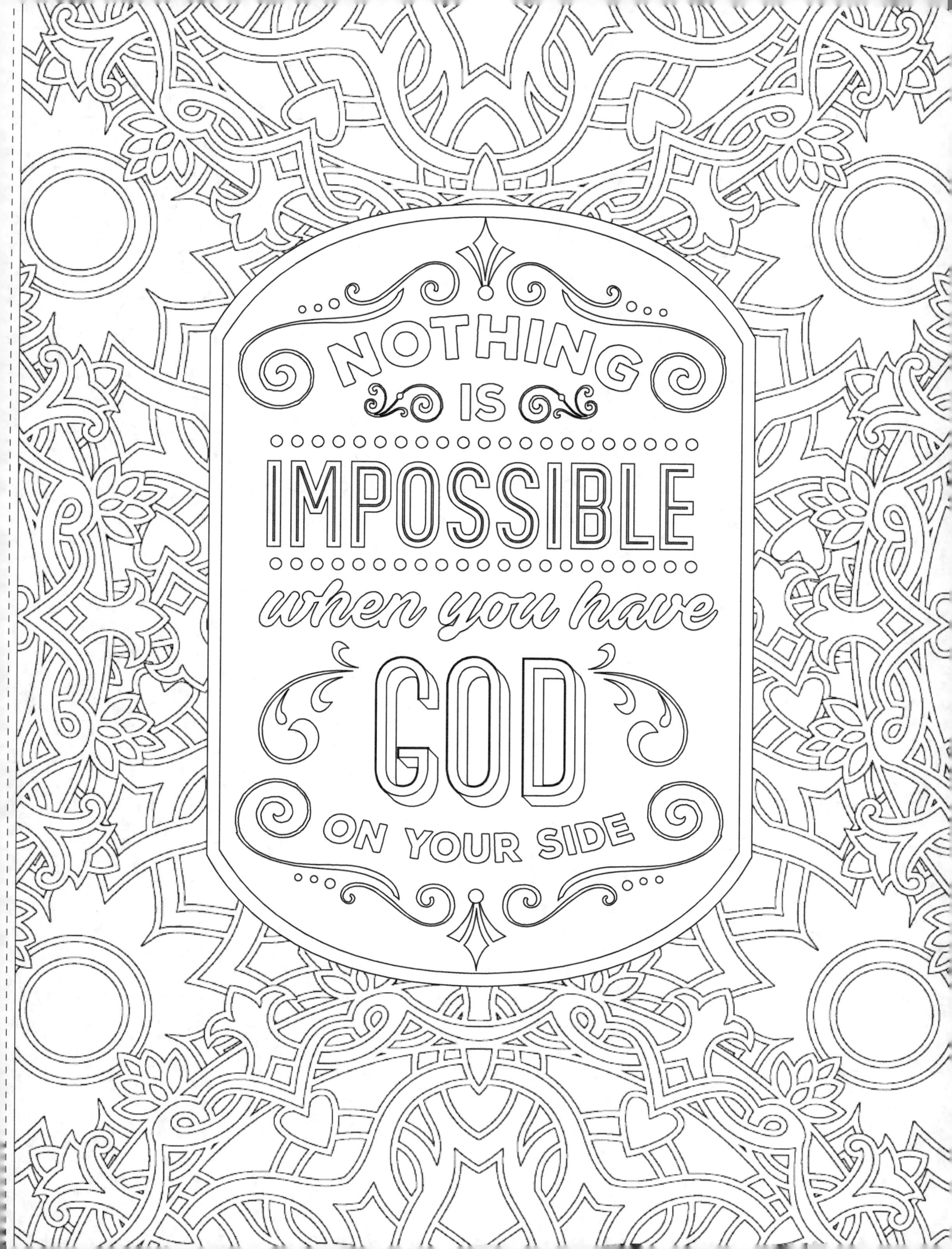

NOTHING
IS
IMPOSSIBLE
when you have
GOD
ON YOUR SIDE

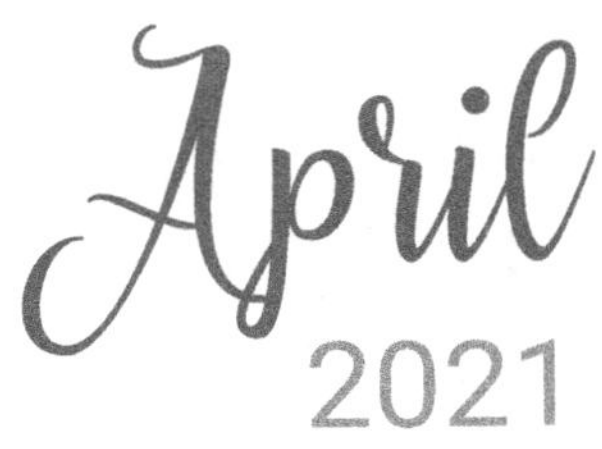

April
2021

19 MONDAY

20 TUESDAY

21 WEDNESDAY

22 THURSDAY Earth Day

23 FRIDAY

24 SATURDAY

25 SUNDAY

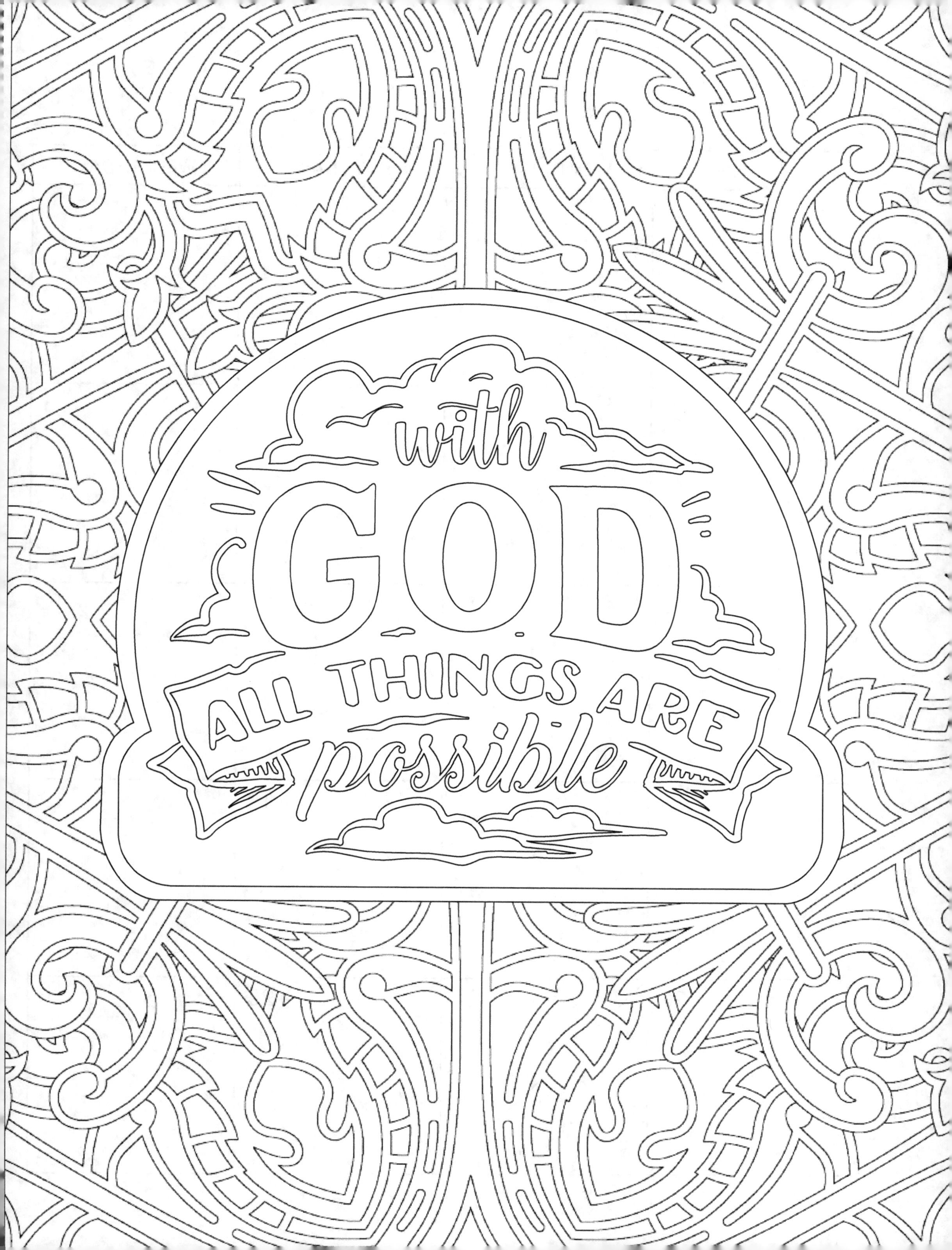
with
GOD
ALL THINGS ARE
possible

May 2021

SUNDAY	MONDAY	TUESDAY	WEDNESDAY
2	3	4	5
9 Mother's Day	10	11	12
16	17	18	19
23 30	24 31 Memorial Day	25	26

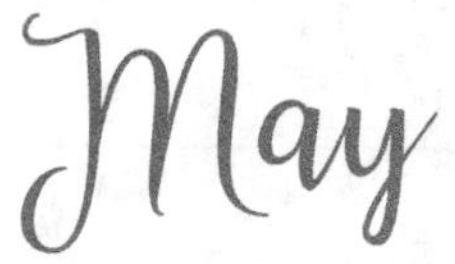

May

THURSDAY	FRIDAY	SATURDAY	NOTES
		1	○
			○
			○
			○
			○
6	7	8	○
			○
			○
			○
13	14	15	○
			○
			○
			○
			○
20	21	22	○
			○
			○
			○
			○
27	28	29	NOTES

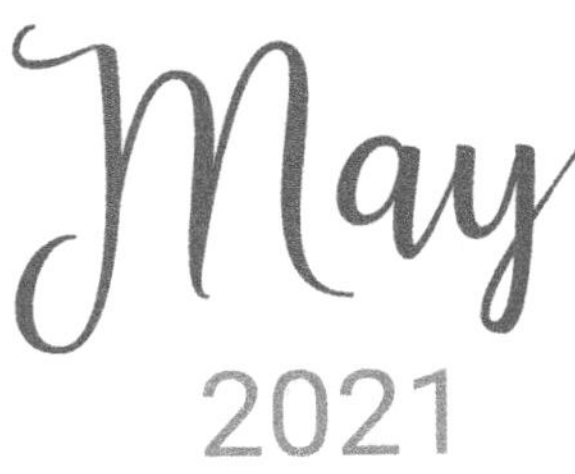

May
2021

26 MONDAY

27 TUESDAY

28 WEDNESDAY

29 THURSDAY

30 FRIDAY

01 SATURDAY

02 SUNDAY

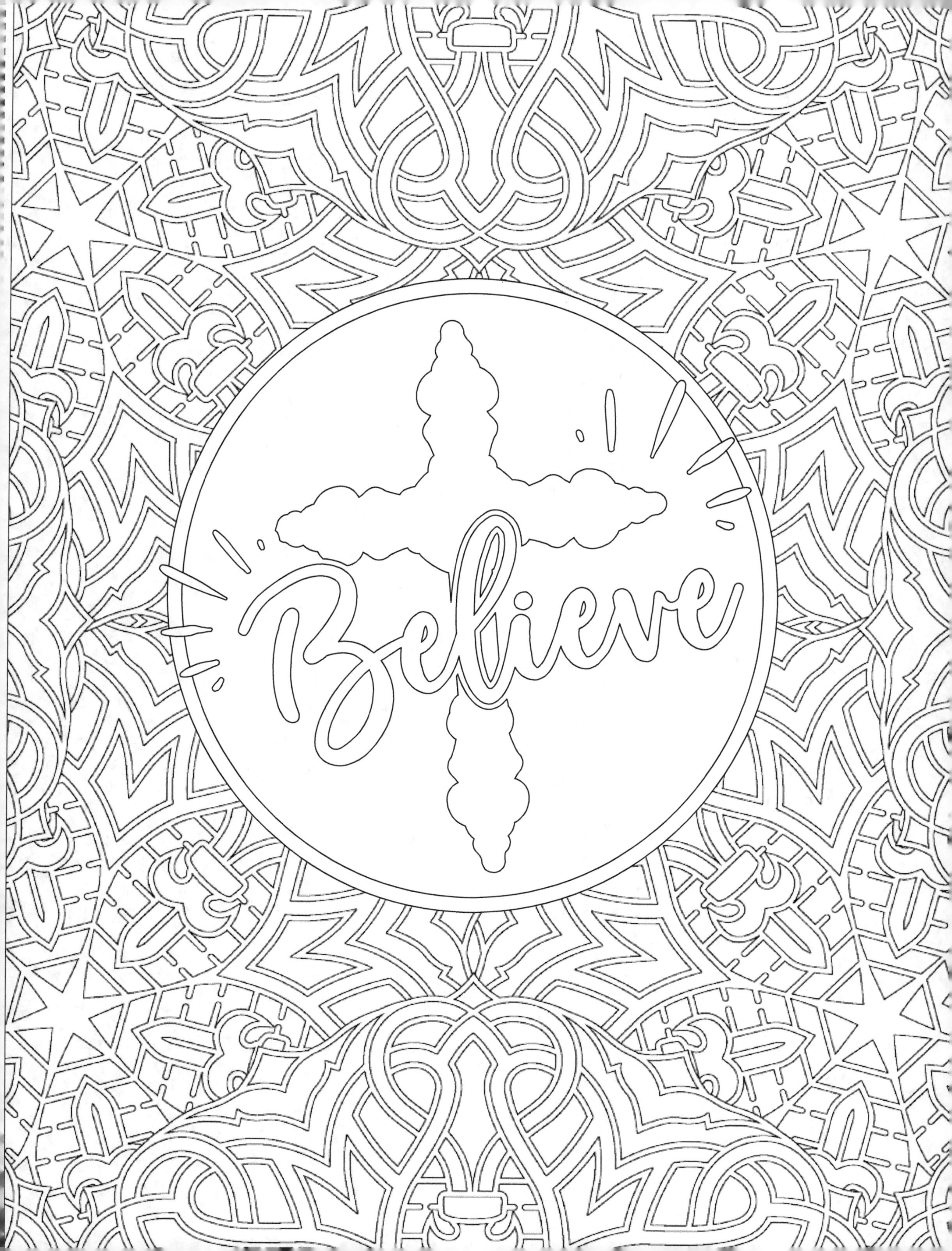

Believe

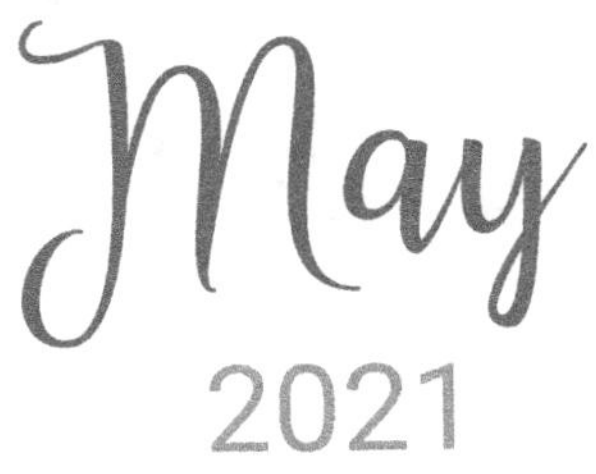

May
2021

03 MONDAY

04 TUESDAY

05 WEDNESDAY

06 THURSDAY

07 FRIDAY

08 SATURDAY

09 SUNDAY   Mother's Day

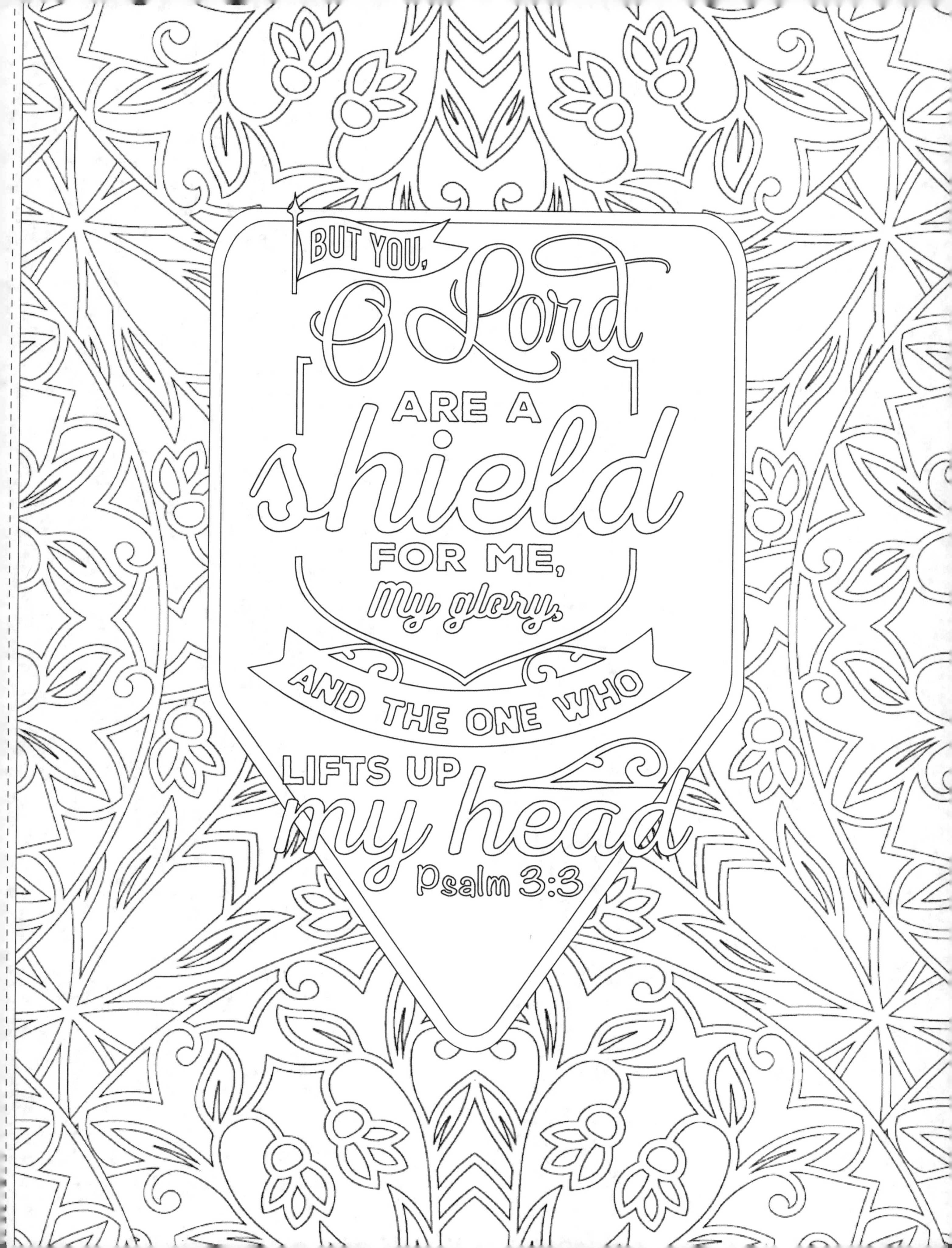
BUT YOU,
O Lord
ARE A
shield
FOR ME,
My glory,
AND THE ONE WHO
LIFTS UP
my head
Psalm 3:3

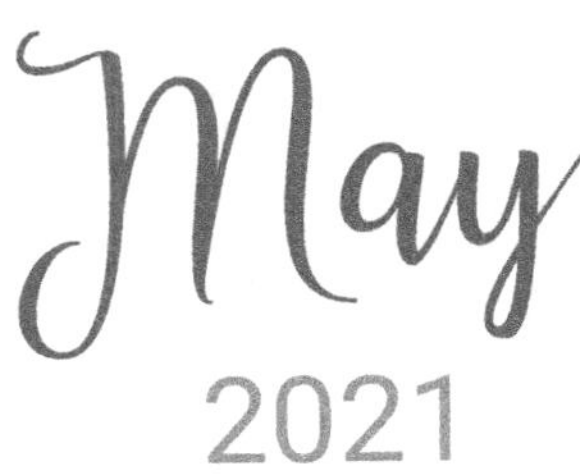

May
2021

10 MONDAY

11 TUESDAY

12 WEDNESDAY

13 THURSDAY

14 FRIDAY

15 SATURDAY

16 SUNDAY

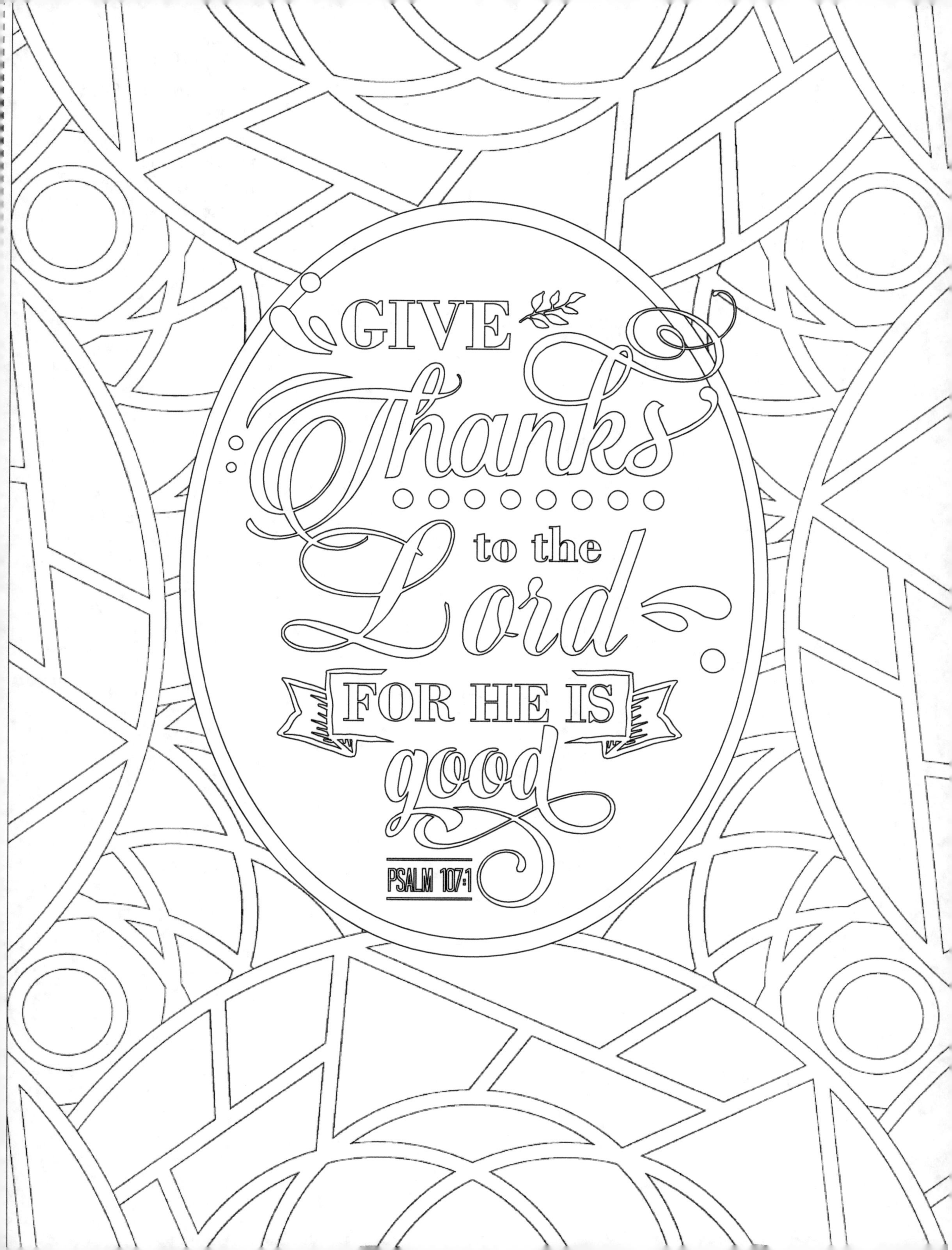

GIVE
Thanks
to the
Lord
FOR HE IS
good
PSALM 107:1

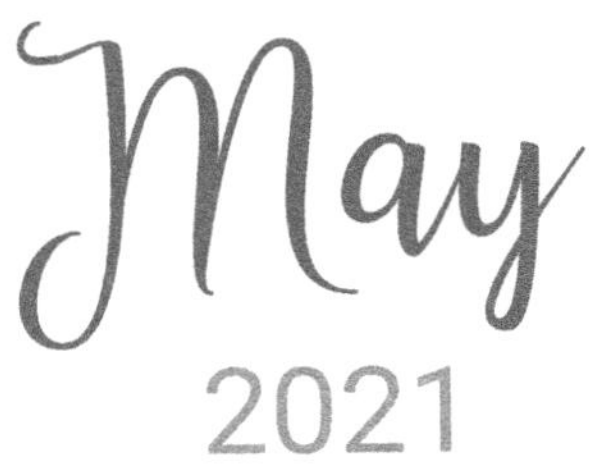

May
2021

17 MONDAY

18 TUESDAY

19 WEDNESDAY

20 THURSDAY

21 FRIDAY

22 SATURDAY

23 SUNDAY

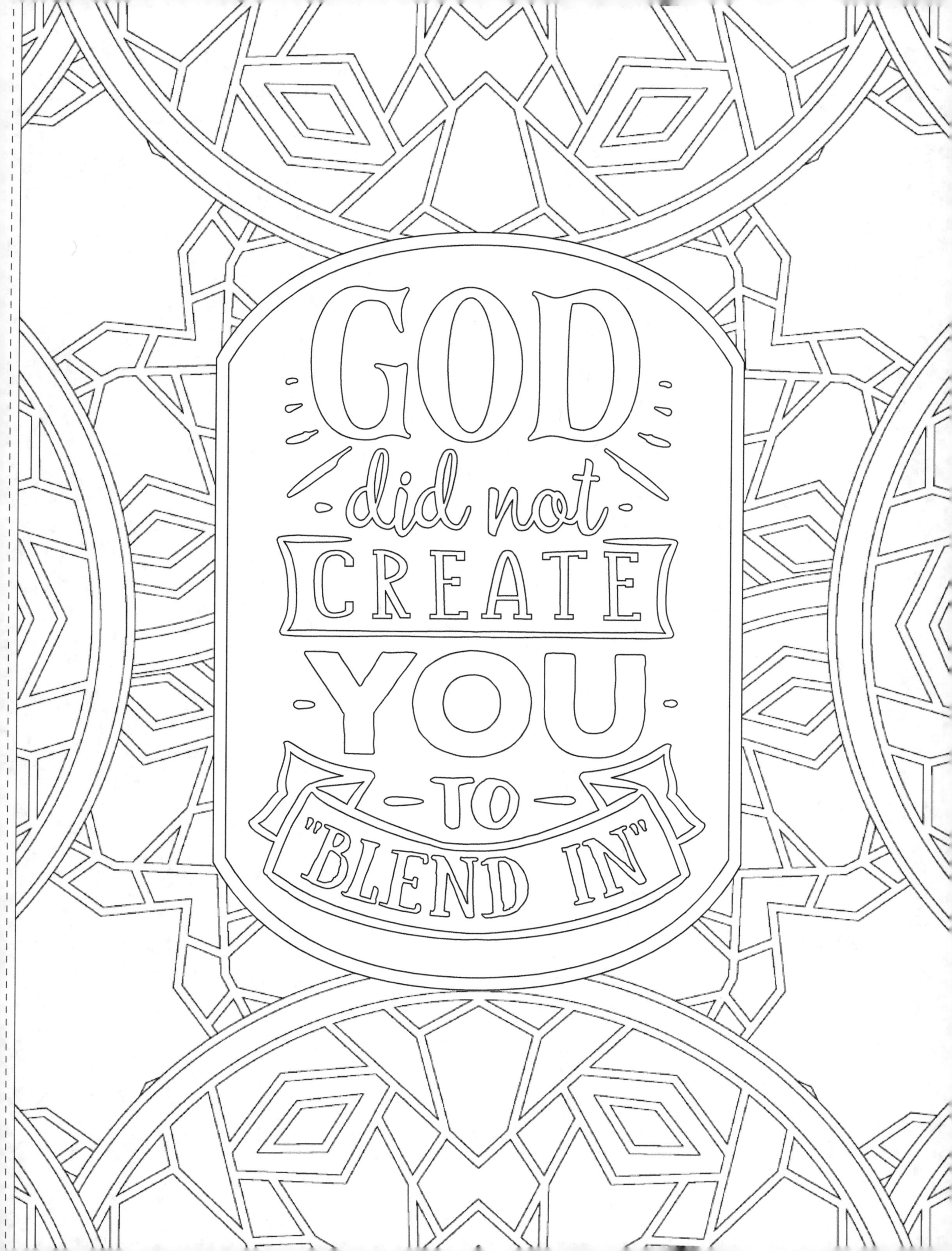

GOD
did not
CREATE
YOU
TO
"BLEND IN"

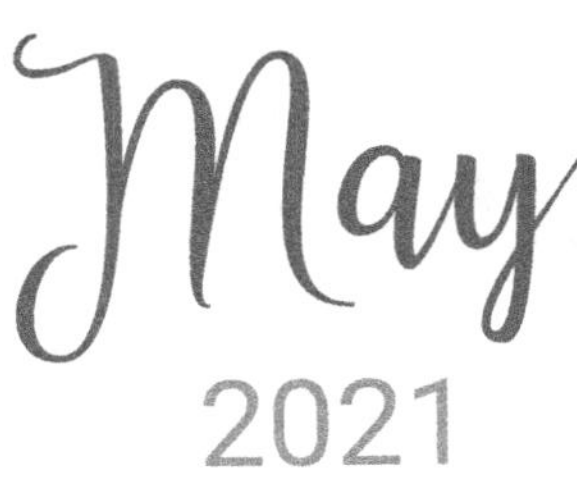

May
2021

24 MONDAY

25 TUESDAY

26 WEDNESDAY

27 THURSDAY

28 FRIDAY

29 SATURDAY

30 SUNDAY

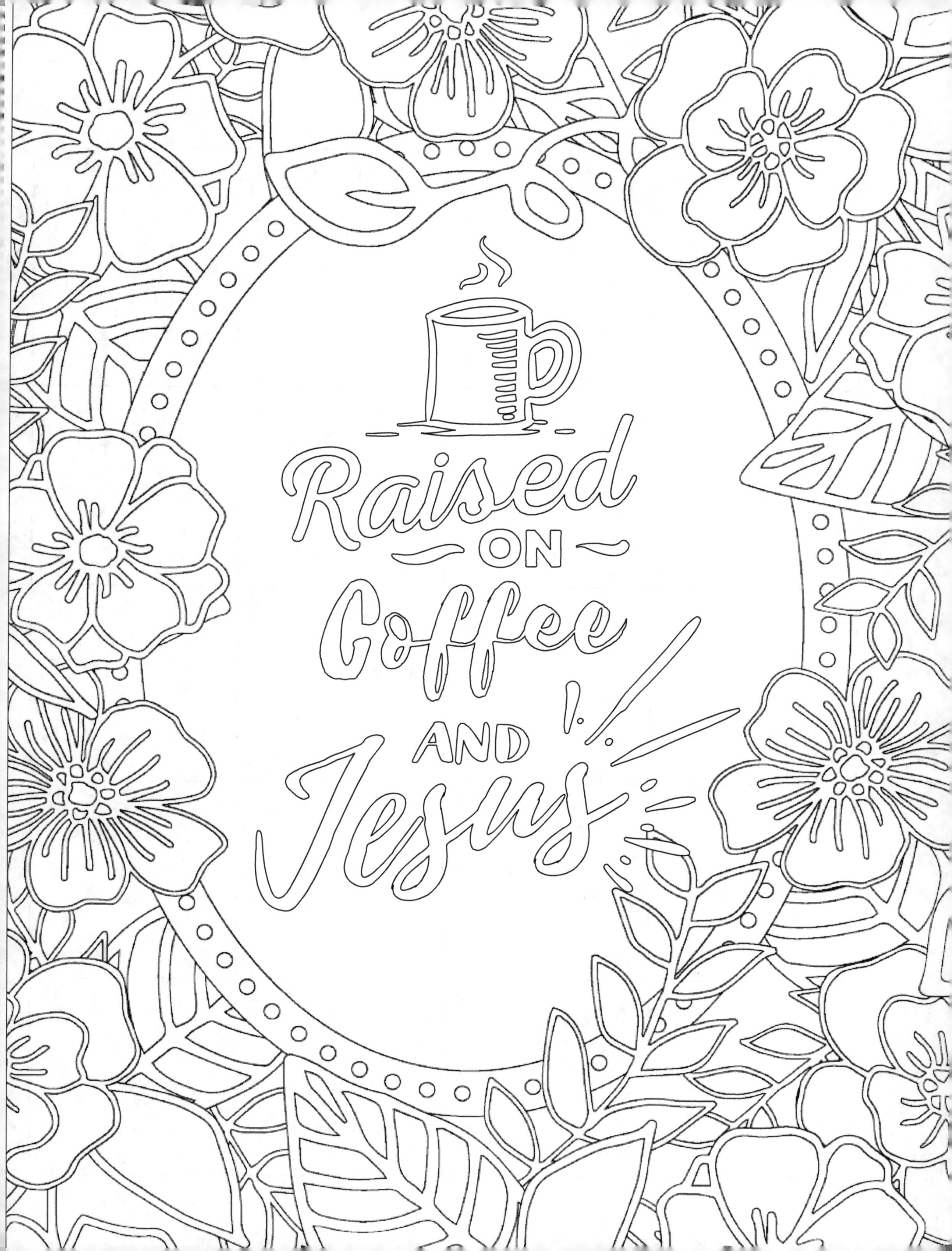

Raised
ON
Coffee
AND
Jesus

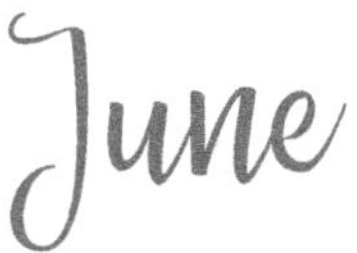

June 2021

SUNDAY	MONDAY	TUESDAY	WEDNESDAY
		1	2
6	7	8	9
13	14 Flag Day	15	16
20 Father's Day	21 First Day of Summer	22	23
27	28	29	30

June 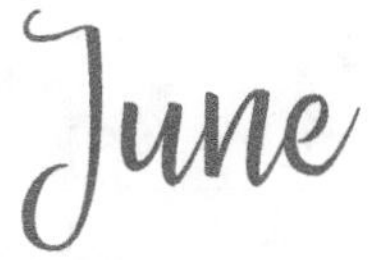 2021

THURSDAY	FRIDAY	SATURDAY	NOTES
3	4	5	○
			○
			○
			○
			○
10	11	12	○
			○
			○
			○
17	18	19	○
			○
			○
			○
24	25	26	○
			○
			○
			○
			○
			NOTES

June
2021

June

S	M	T	W	T	F	S
		1	2	3	4	5
6	7	8	9	10	11	12
13	14	15	16	17	18	19
20	21	22	23	24	25	26
27	28	29	30			

31 MONDAY   Memorial Day

01 TUESDAY

02 WEDNESDAY

03 THURSDAY

04 FRIDAY

05 SATURDAY

06 SUNDAY

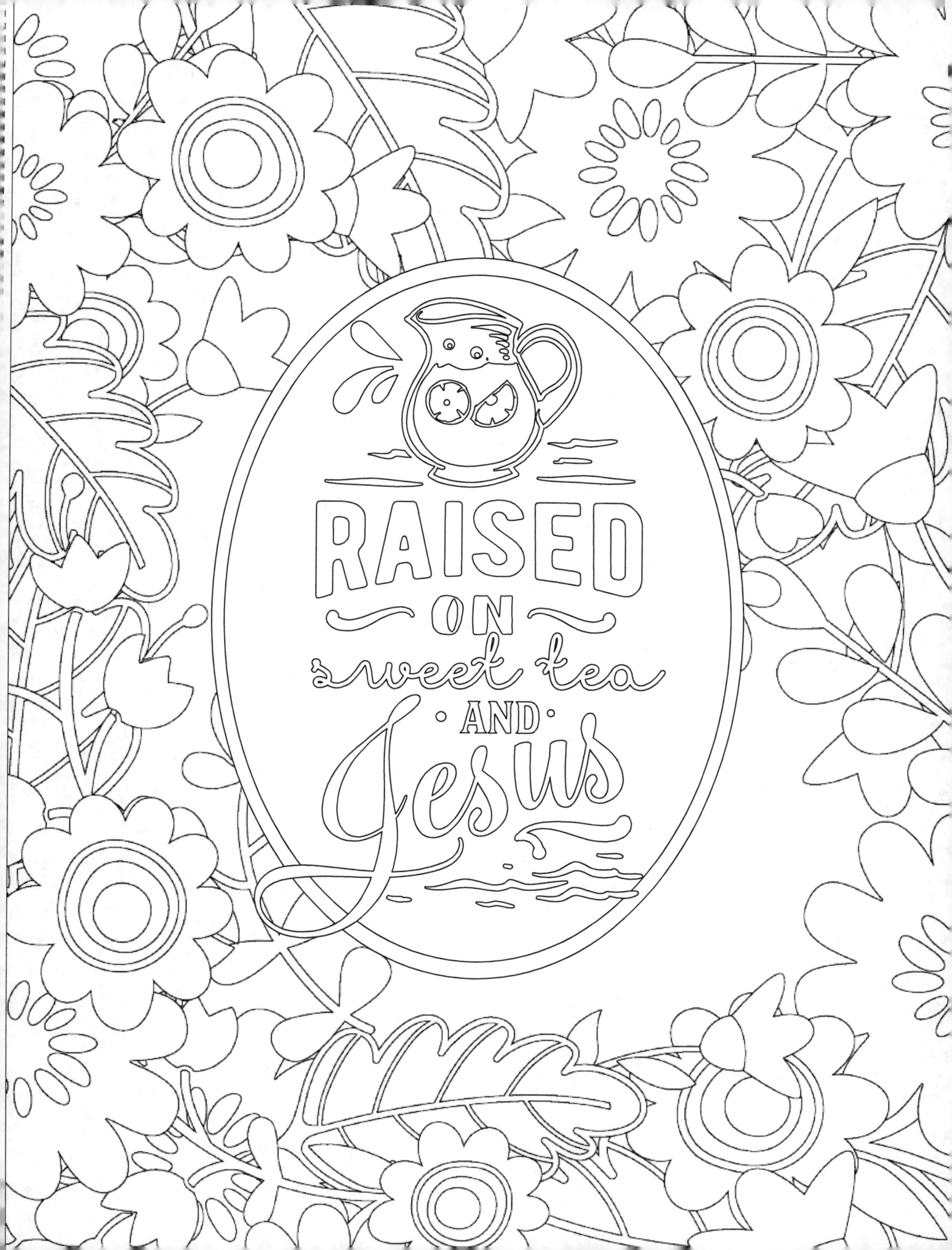

RAISED
ON
sweet tea
AND
Jesus

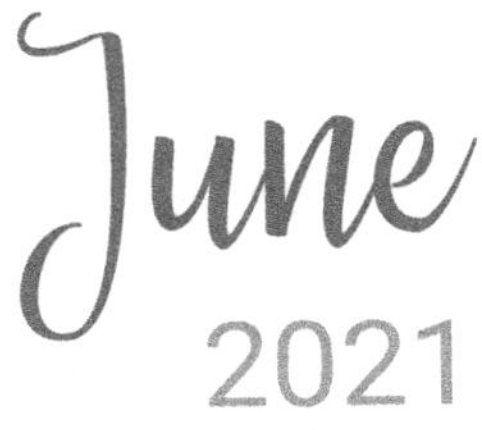

June
2021

07 MONDAY

08 TUESDAY

09 WEDNESDAY

10 THURSDAY

11 FRIDAY

12 SATURDAY

13 SUNDAY

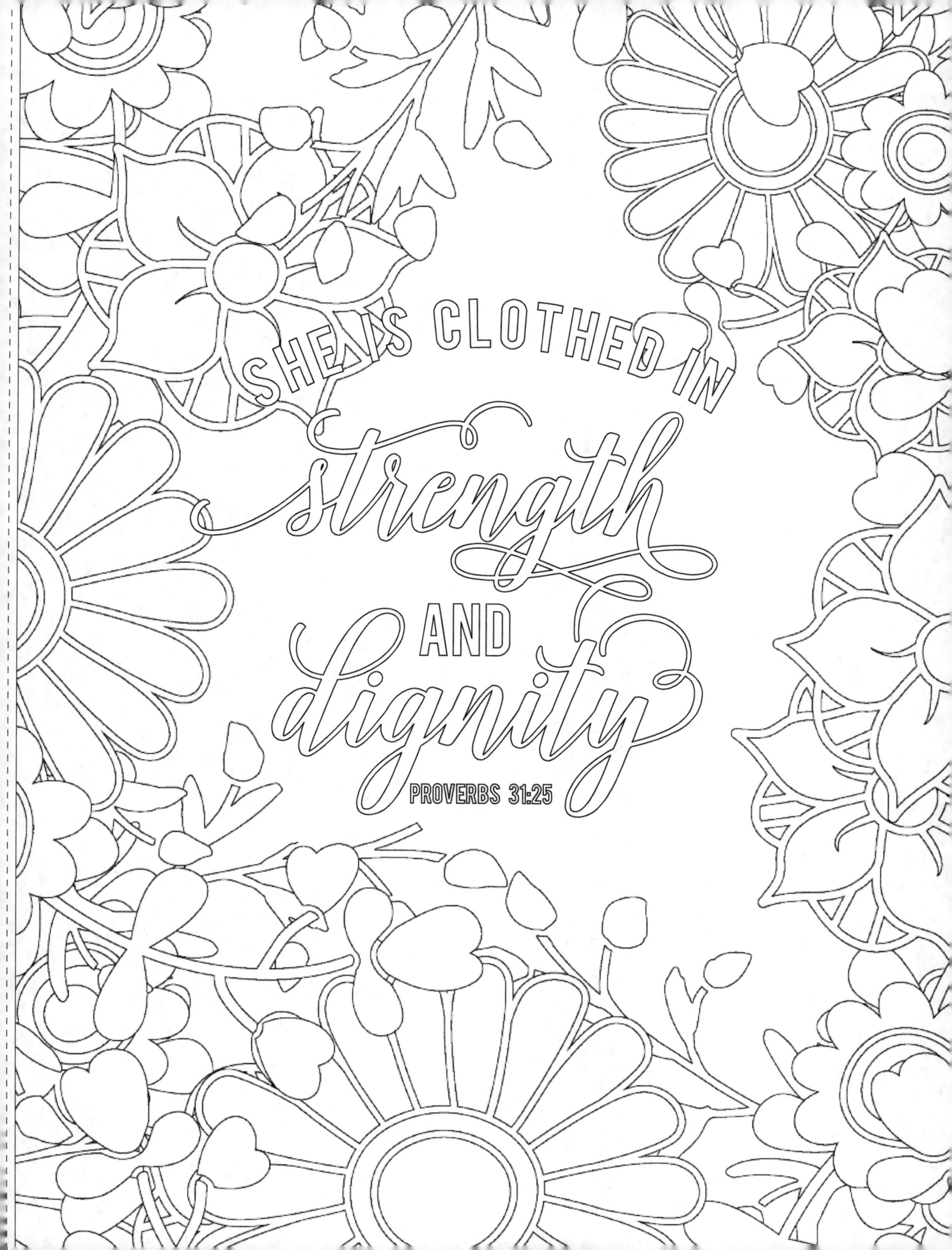

SHE IS CLOTHED IN
strength
AND
dignity
PROVERBS 31:25

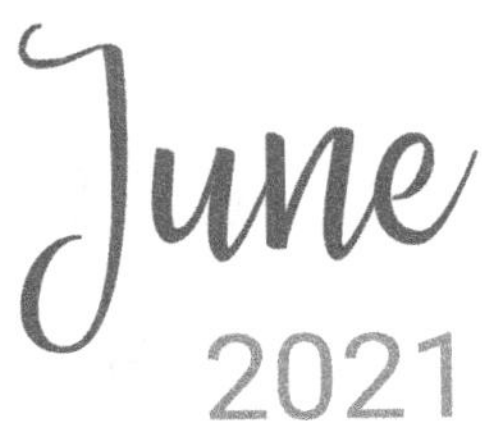

June
2021

14 MONDAY Flag Day

15 TUESDAY

16 WEDNESDAY

17 THURSDAY

18 FRIDAY

19 SATURDAY

20 SUNDAY Father's Day

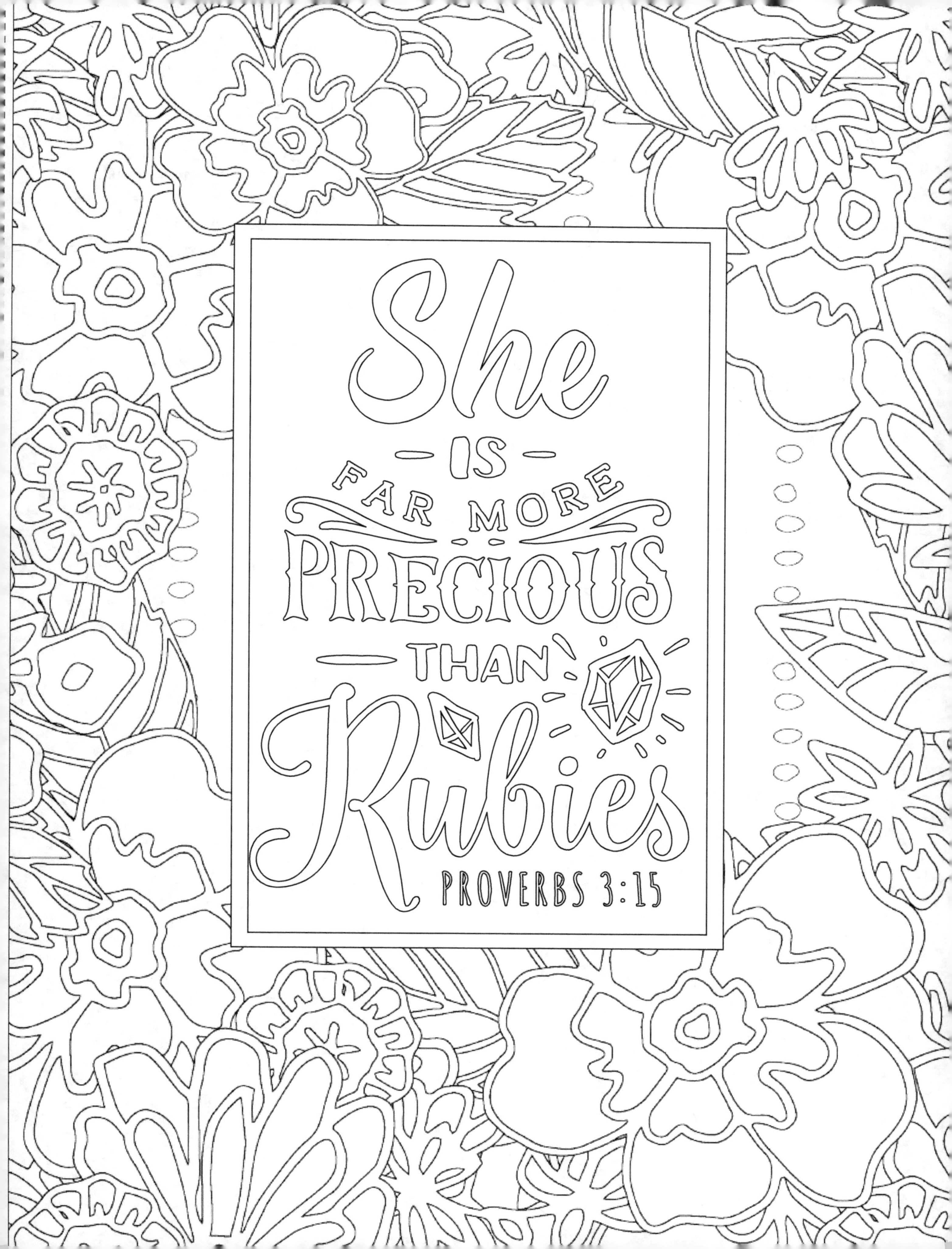

She
- IS -
FAR MORE
PRECIOUS
- THAN -
Rubies
PROVERBS 3:15

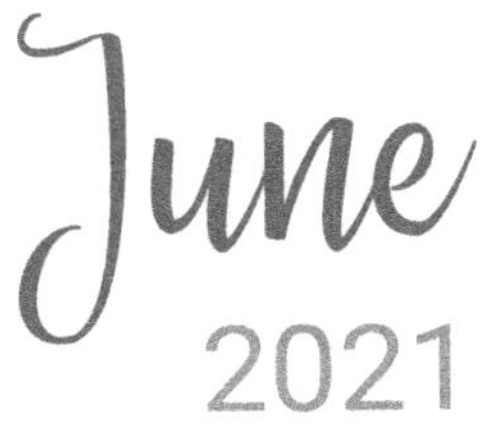

June
2021

21 MONDAY First Day of Summer

22 TUESDAY

23 WEDNESDAY

24 THURSDAY

25 FRIDAY

26 SATURDAY

27 SUNDAY

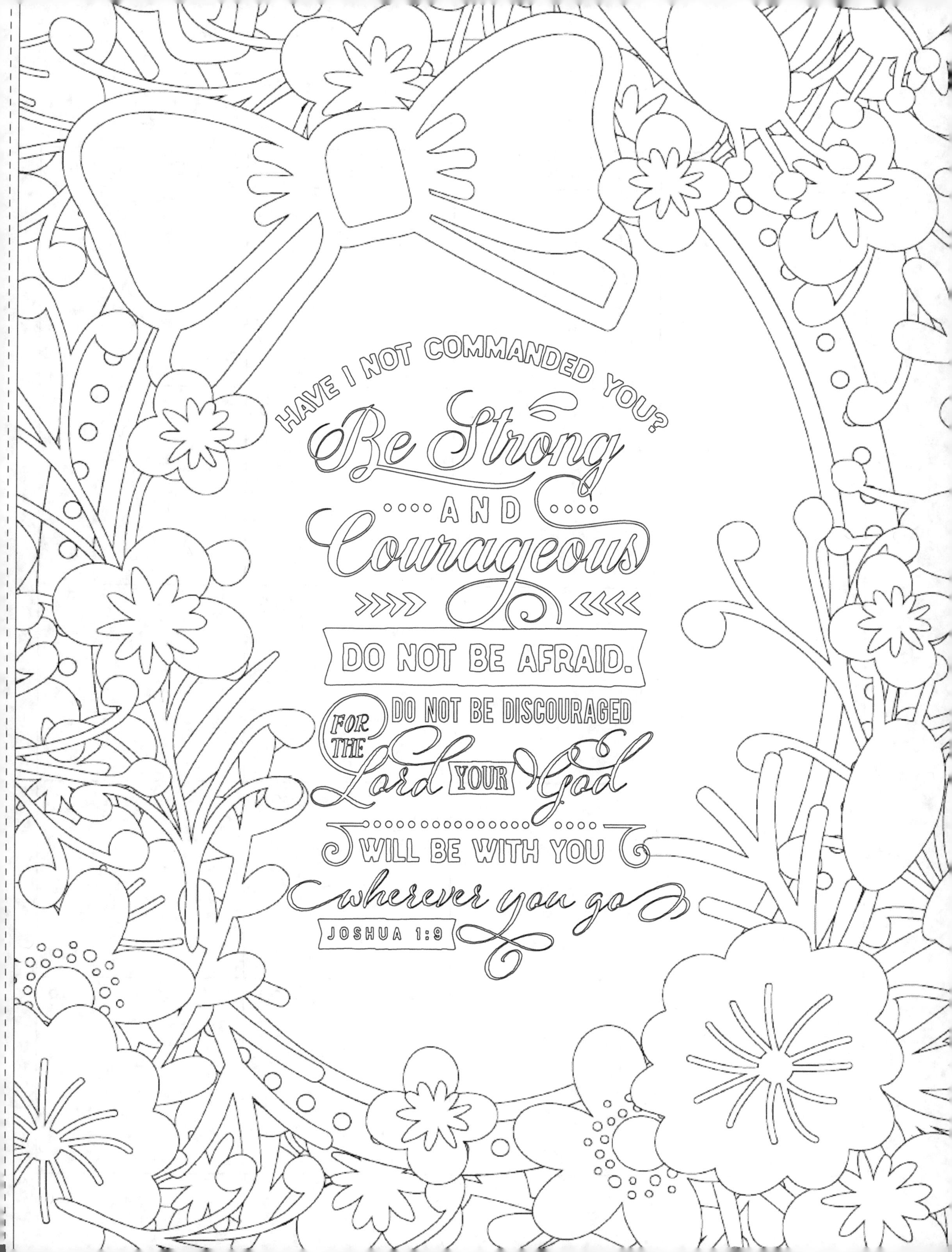

HAVE I NOT COMMANDED YOU?
Be Strong
AND
Courageous
DO NOT BE AFRAID.
FOR THE
DO NOT BE DISCOURAGED
Lord YOUR God
WILL BE WITH YOU
wherever you go
JOSHUA 1:9

SUNDAY	MONDAY	TUESDAY	WEDNESDAY
4 Independence Day	5	6	7
11	12	13	14
18	19	20	21
25	26	27	28

July

2021

THURSDAY	FRIDAY	SATURDAY	NOTES
1	2	3	○
			○
			○
			○
			○
8	9	10	○
			○
			○
			○
15	16	17	○
			○
			○
			○
			○
22	23	24	○
			○
			○
			○
			○
29	30		NOTES

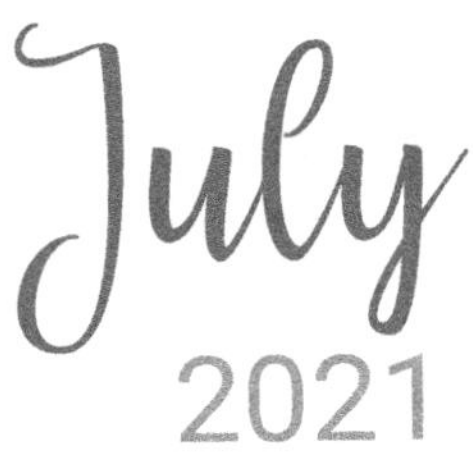

July
2021

28 MONDAY

29 TUESDAY

30 WEDNESDAY

01 THURSDAY

02 FRIDAY

03 SATURDAY

04 SUNDAY   Independence Day

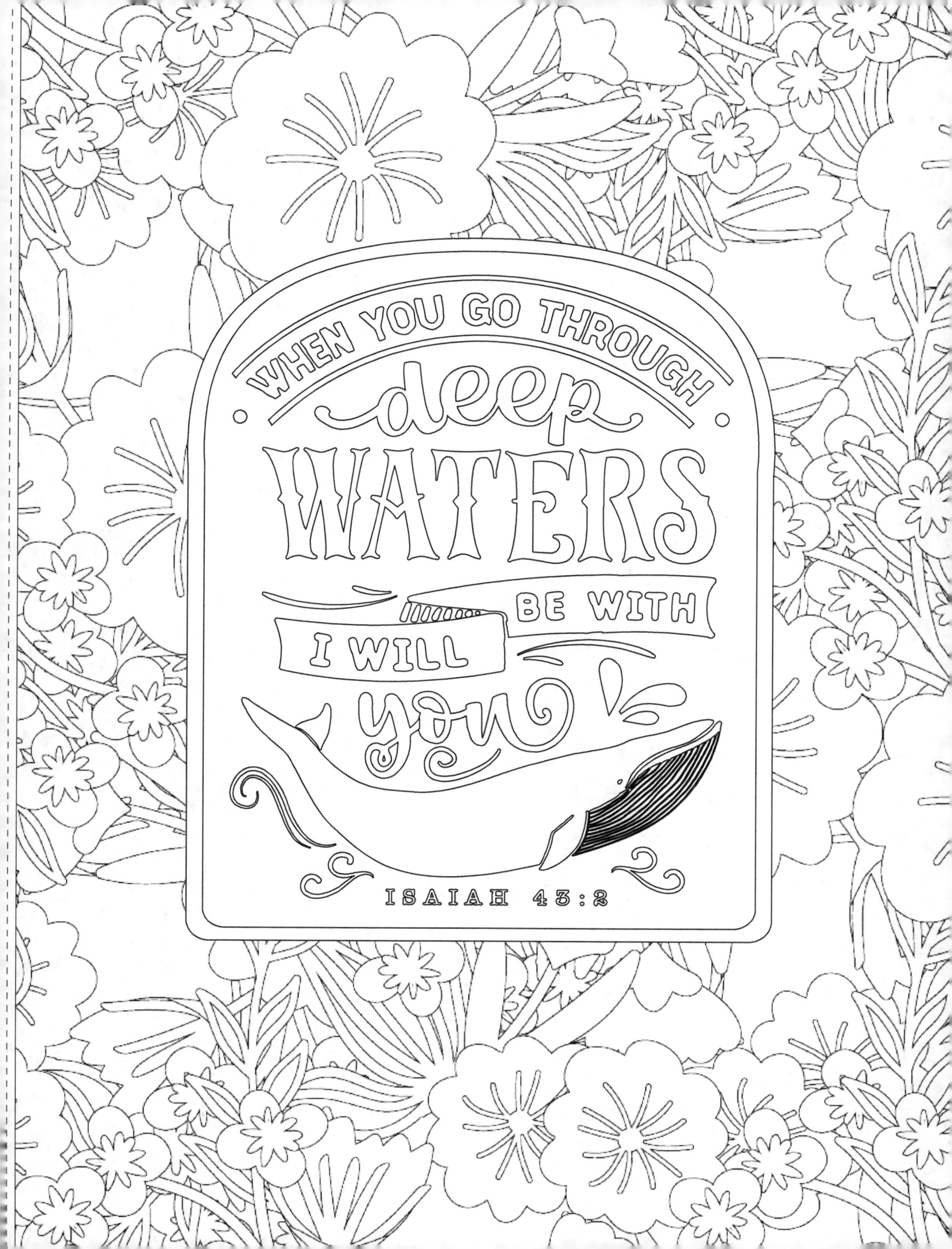

WHEN YOU GO THROUGH
deep
WATERS
I WILL
BE WITH
YOU
ISAIAH 43:2

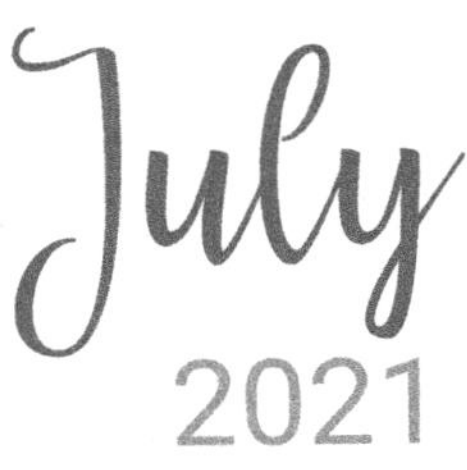

July
2021

05 MONDAY

06 TUESDAY

07 WEDNESDAY

08 THURSDAY

09 FRIDAY

10 SATURDAY

11 SUNDAY

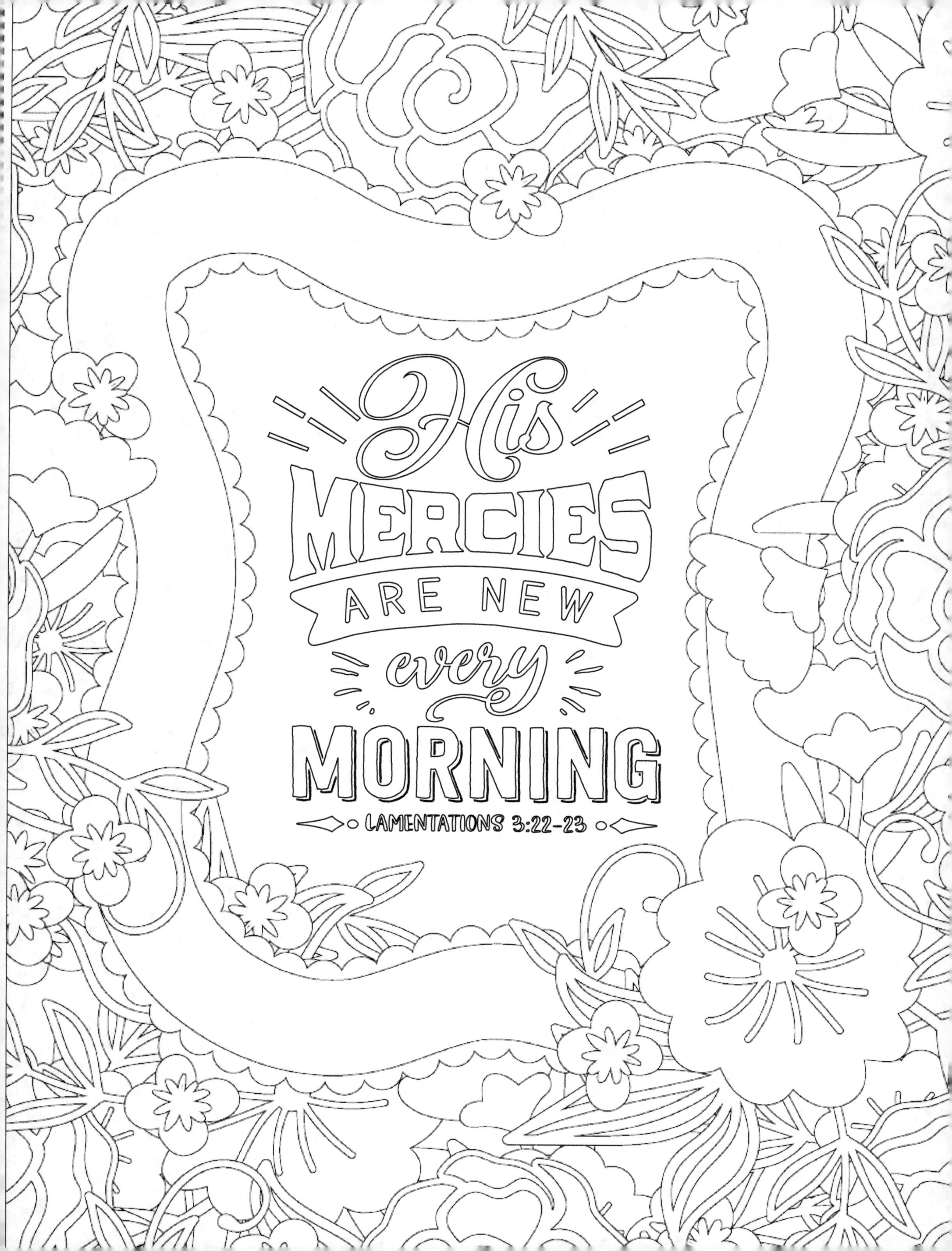

His
MERCIES
ARE NEW
every
MORNING
LAMENTATIONS 3:22-23

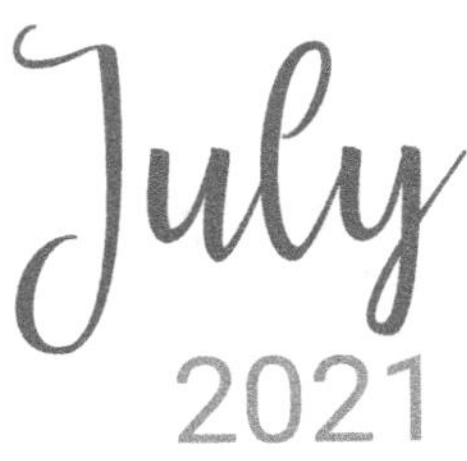

July
2021

12 MONDAY

13 TUESDAY

14 WEDNESDAY

15 THURSDAY

16 FRIDAY

17 SATURDAY

18 SUNDAY

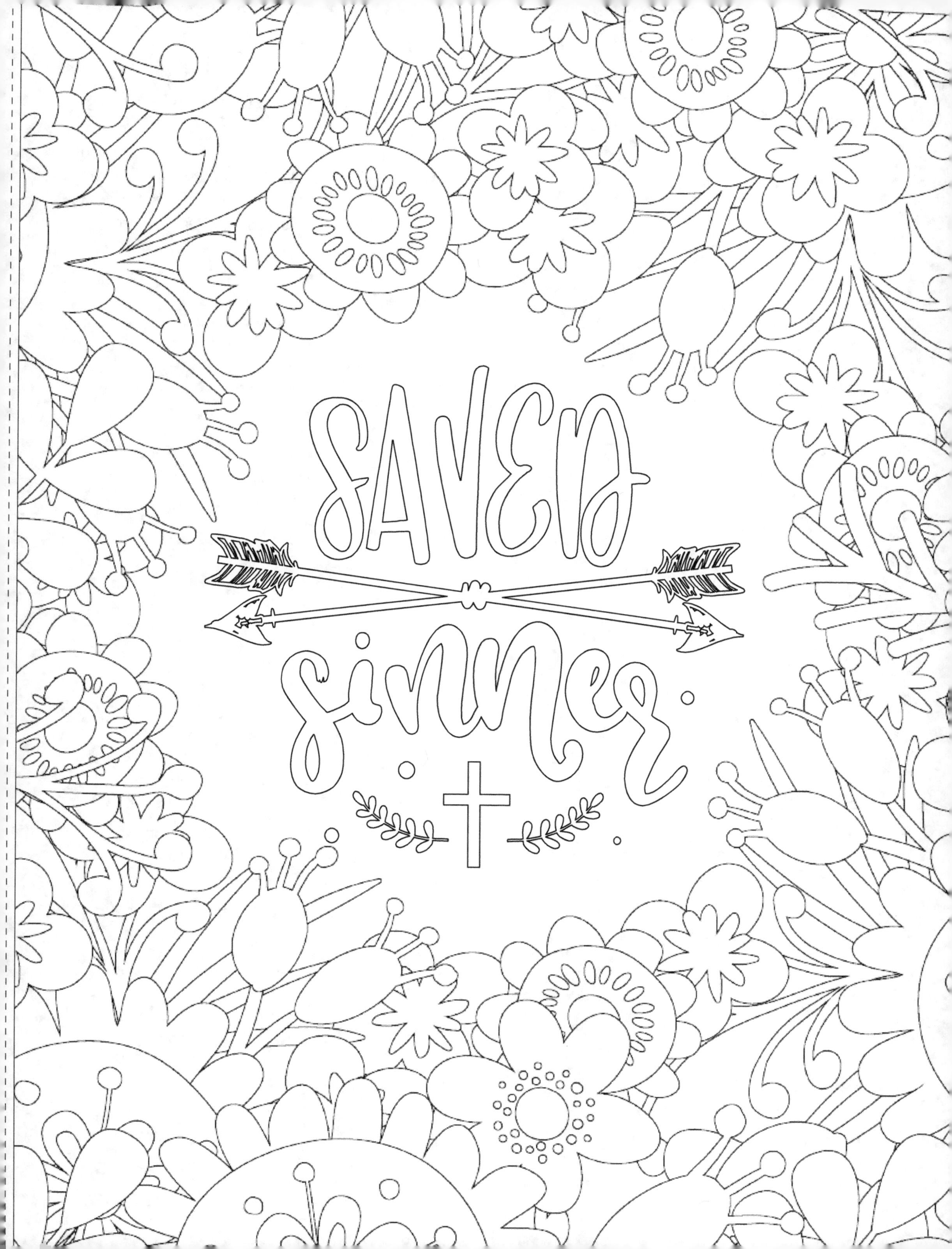

SAVED
sinner

July
2021

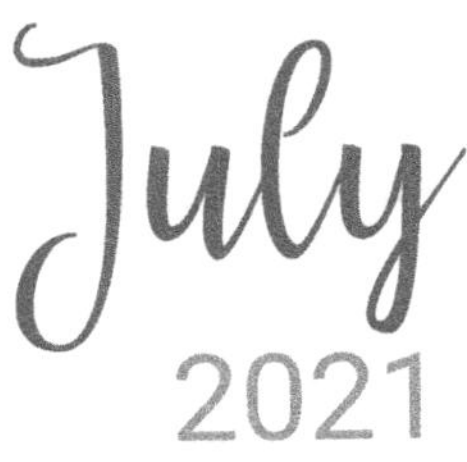

19 MONDAY

20 TUESDAY

21 WEDNESDAY

22 THURSDAY

23 FRIDAY

24 SATURDAY

25 SUNDAY

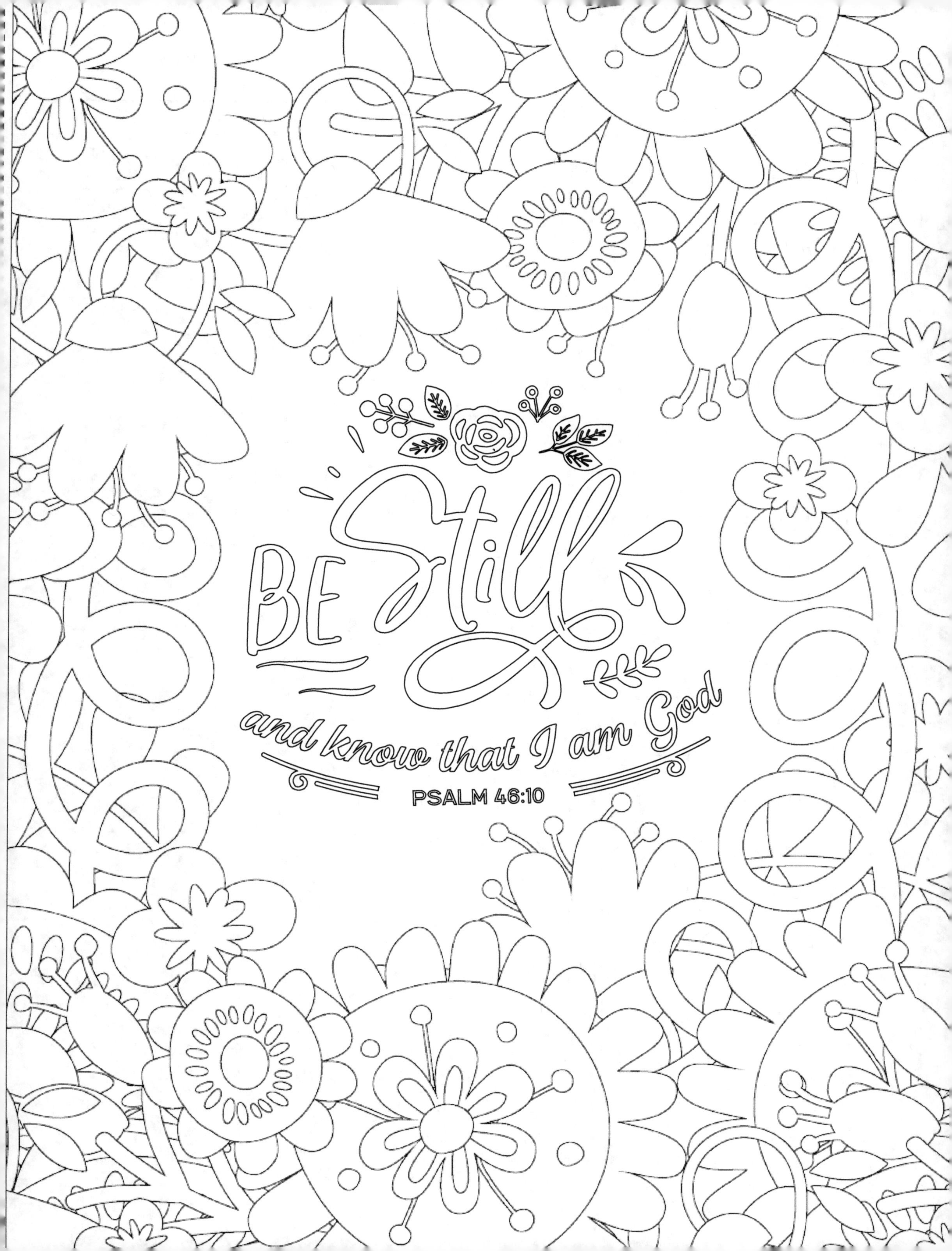

Be Still
and know that I am God
PSALM 46:10

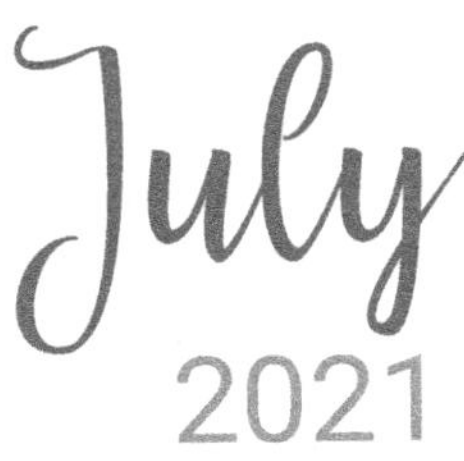

July
2021

26 MONDAY

27 TUESDAY

28 WEDNESDAY

29 THURSDAY

30 FRIDAY

31 SATURDAY

01 SUNDAY

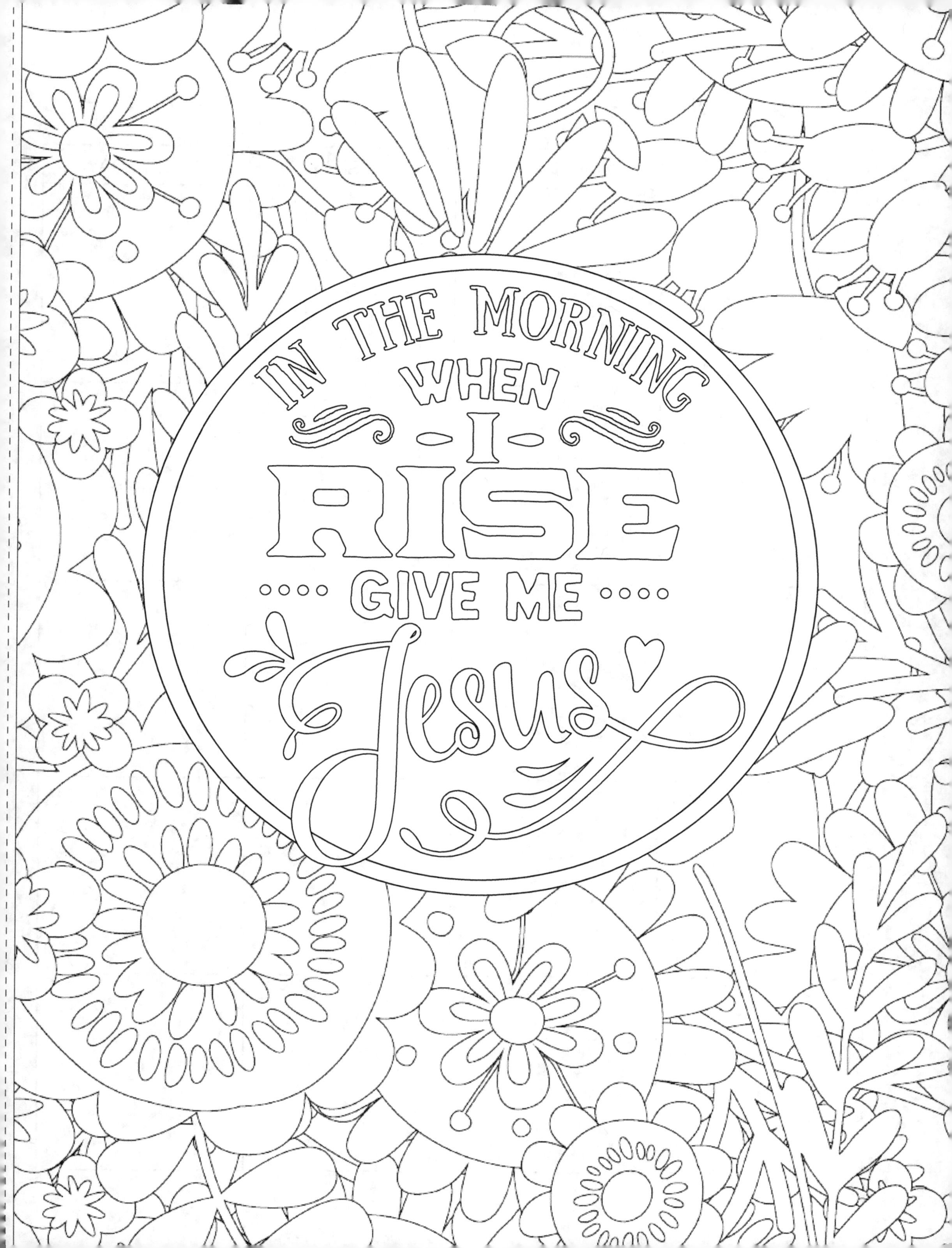

IN THE MORNING
WHEN
I
RISE
GIVE ME
Jesus

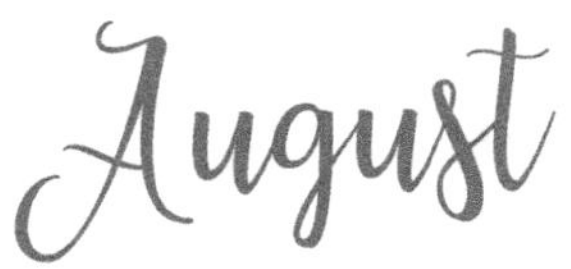

August 2021

SUNDAY	MONDAY	TUESDAY	WEDNESDAY
1	2	3	4
8	9	10	11
15	16	17	18
22	23	24	25
29	30	31	

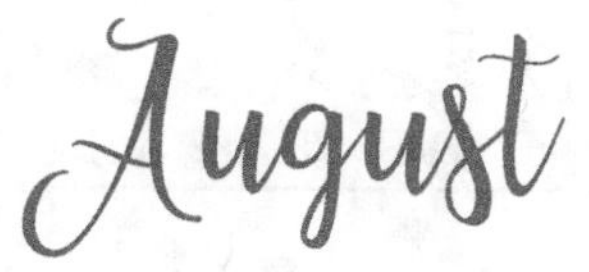

August

THURSDAY	FRIDAY	SATURDAY	NOTES
5	6	7	○
			○
			○
			○
			○
12	13	14	○
			○
			○
			○
19	20	21	○
			○
			○
			○
			○
26	27	28	○
			○
			○
			○
			○
			NOTES

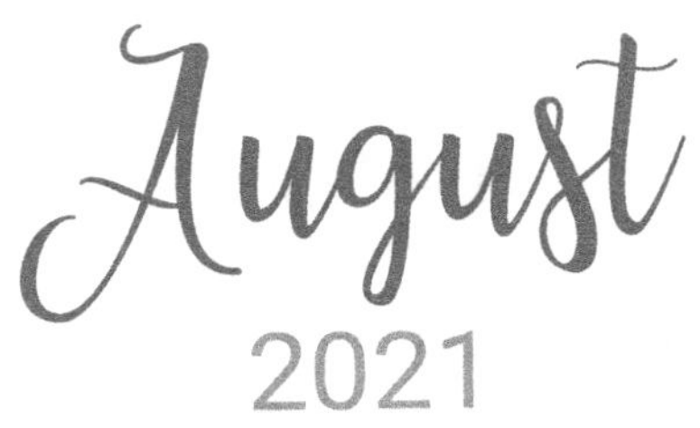

August
2021

02 MONDAY

03 TUESDAY

04 WEDNESDAY

05 THURSDAY

06 FRIDAY

07 SATURDAY

08 SUNDAY

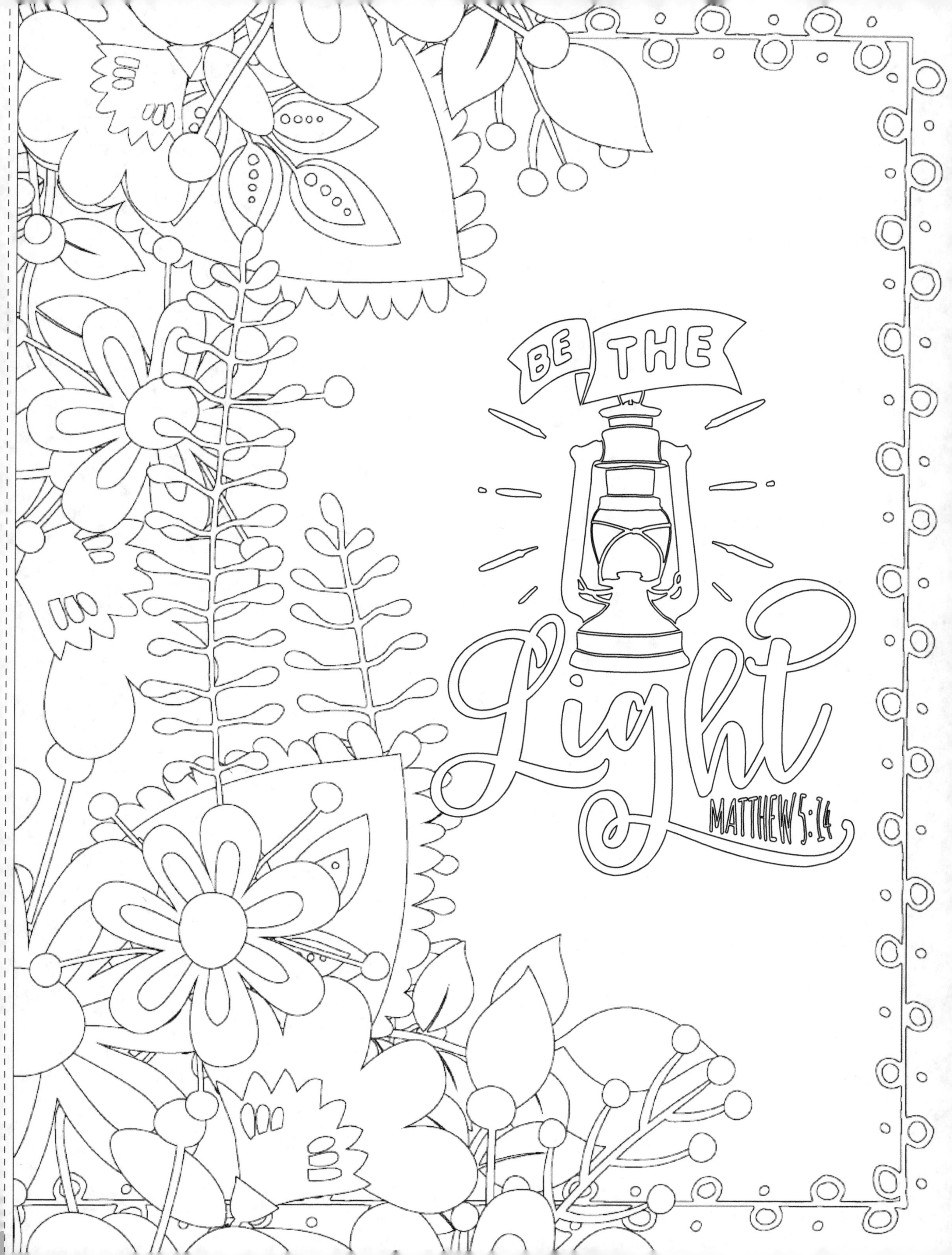

BE THE
Light
MATTHEW 5:14

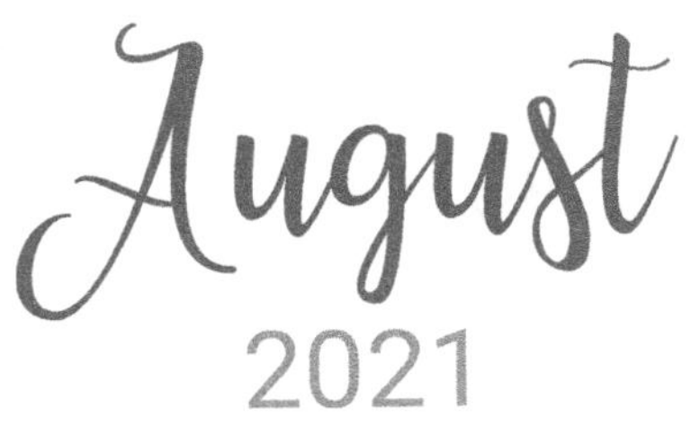

August
2021

09 MONDAY

10 TUESDAY

11 WEDNESDAY

12 THURSDAY

13 FRIDAY

14 SATURDAY

15 SUNDAY

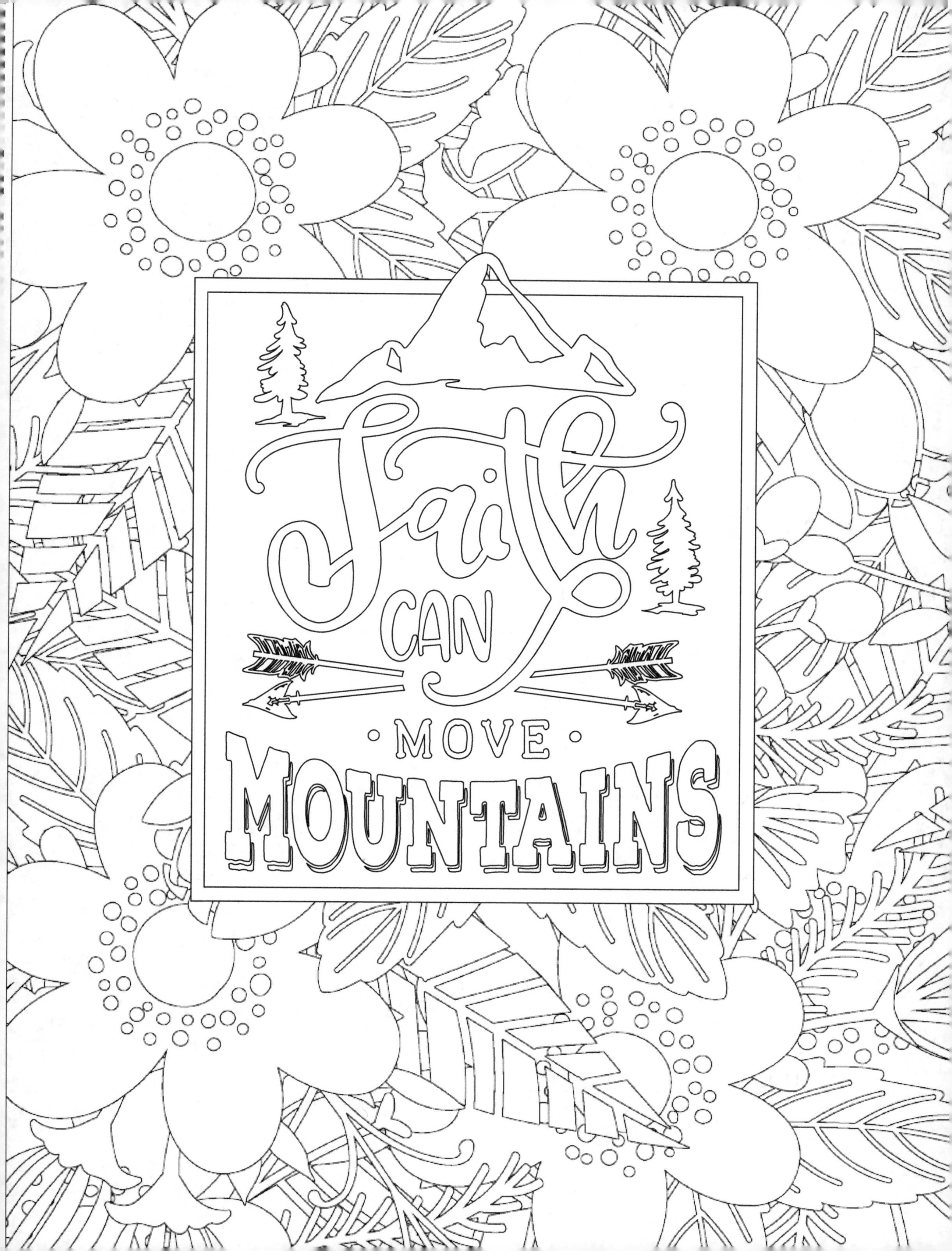

Faith
CAN
·MOVE·
MOUNTAINS

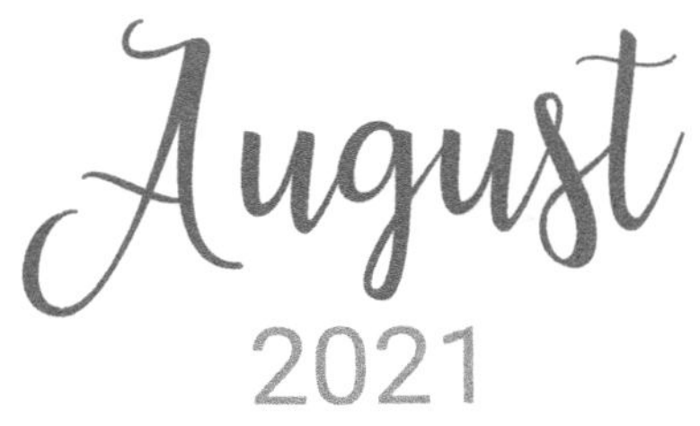

August
2021

16 MONDAY

17 TUESDAY

18 WEDNESDAY

19 THURSDAY

20 FRIDAY

21 SATURDAY

22 SUNDAY

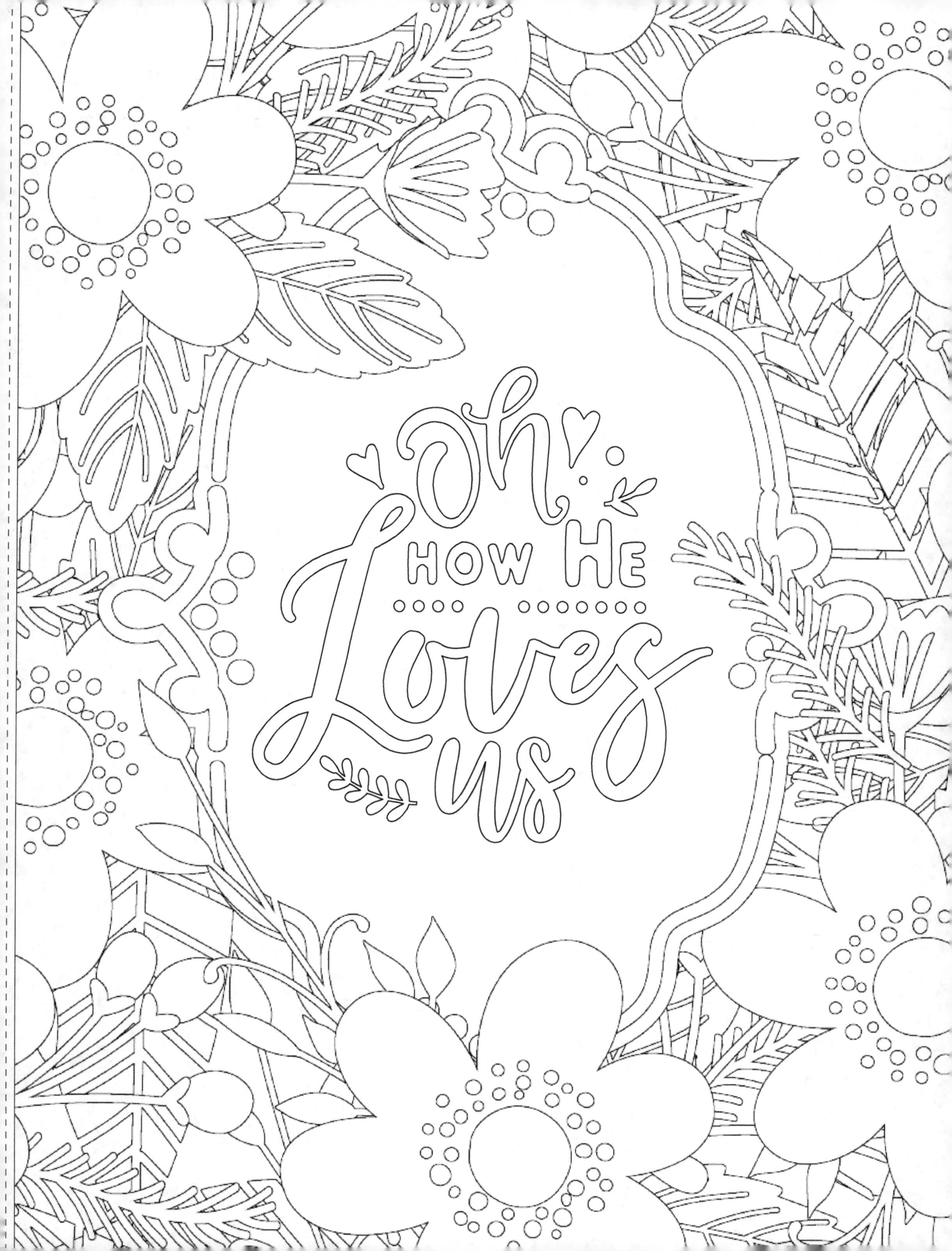

Oh!
how He
Loves
us

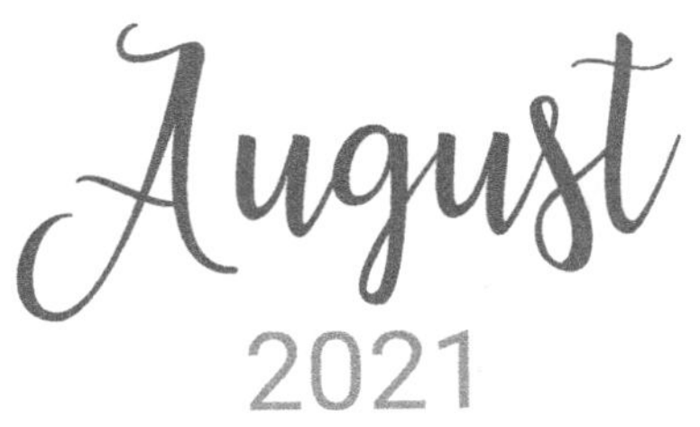

August
2021

23 MONDAY

24 TUESDAY

25 WEDNESDAY

26 THURSDAY

27 FRIDAY

28 SATURDAY

29 SUNDAY

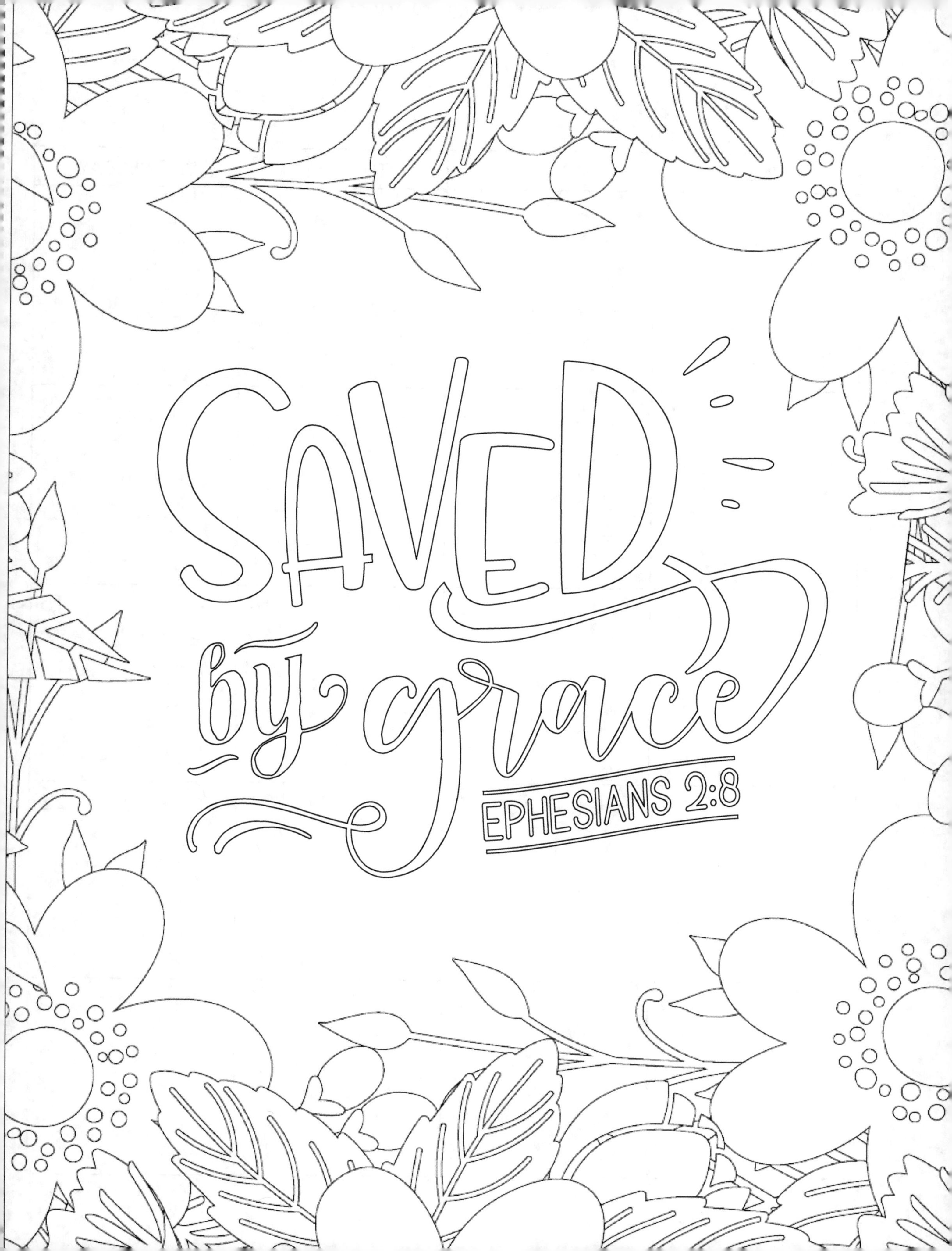

SAVED
by grace
EPHESIANS 2:8

SUNDAY	MONDAY	TUESDAY	WEDNESDAY
			1
5	**6** Labor Day Rosh Hashanah Begins	**7** Rosh Hashanah Ends	**8**
12	**13**	**14**	**15** Yom Kippur Begins
19	**20**	**21**	**22** First Day of Autumn
26	**27**	**28**	**29**

THURSDAY	FRIDAY	SATURDAY	NOTES
2	3	4	○
			○
			○
			○
			○
9	10	11	○
			○
			○
			○
16 Yom Kippur Ends	17	18	○
			○
			○
			○
			○
23	24	25	○
			○
			○
			○
			○
30			NOTES

September

2021

30 MONDAY

31 TUESDAY

01 WEDNESDAY

02 THURSDAY

03 FRIDAY

04 SATURDAY

05 SUNDAY

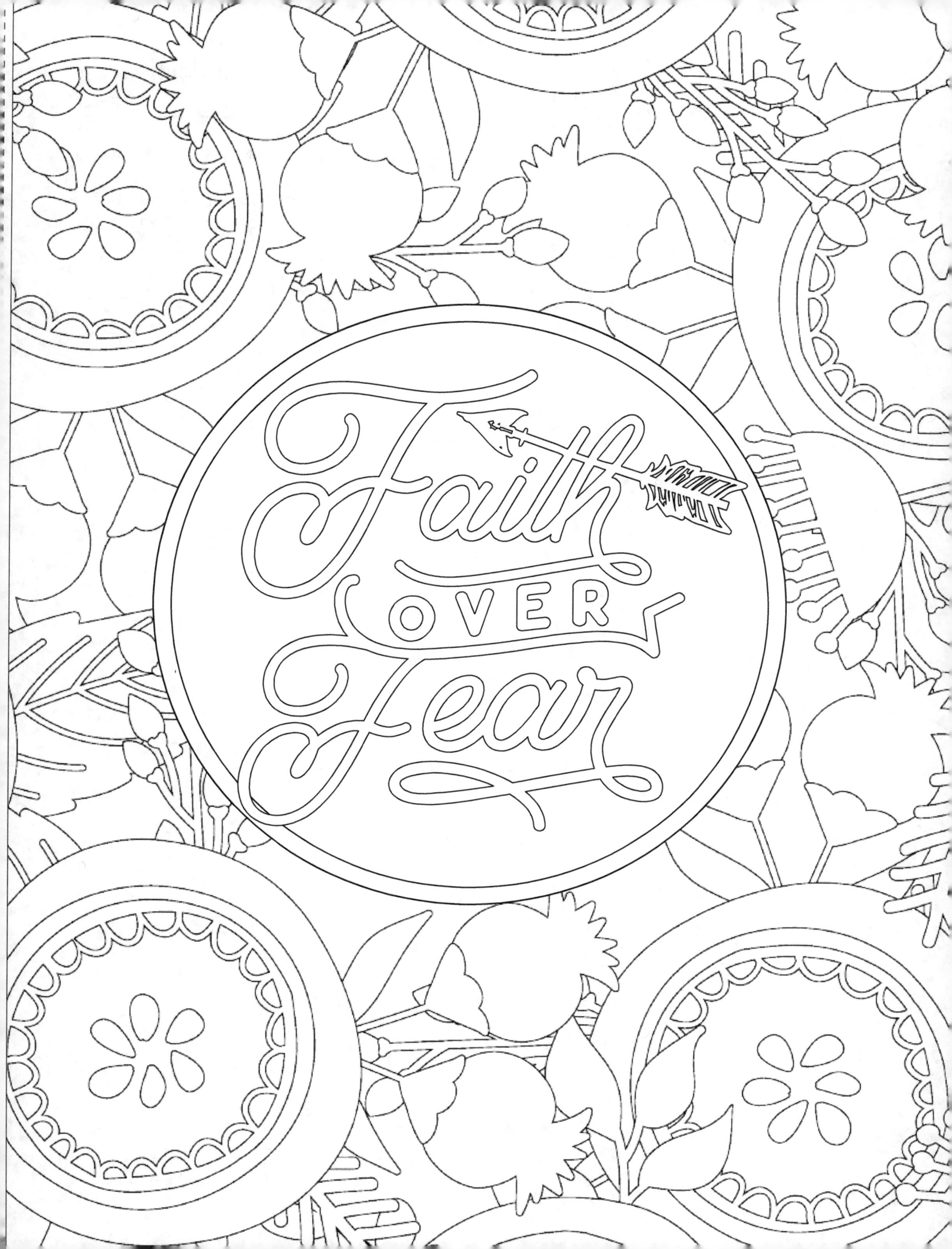

Faith
OVER
Fear

September
2021

06 MONDAY   Labor Day / Rosh Hashanah Begins

07 TUESDAY

08 WEDNESDAY   Rosh Hashanah Ends

09 THURSDAY

10 FRIDAY

11 SATURDAY

12 SUNDAY

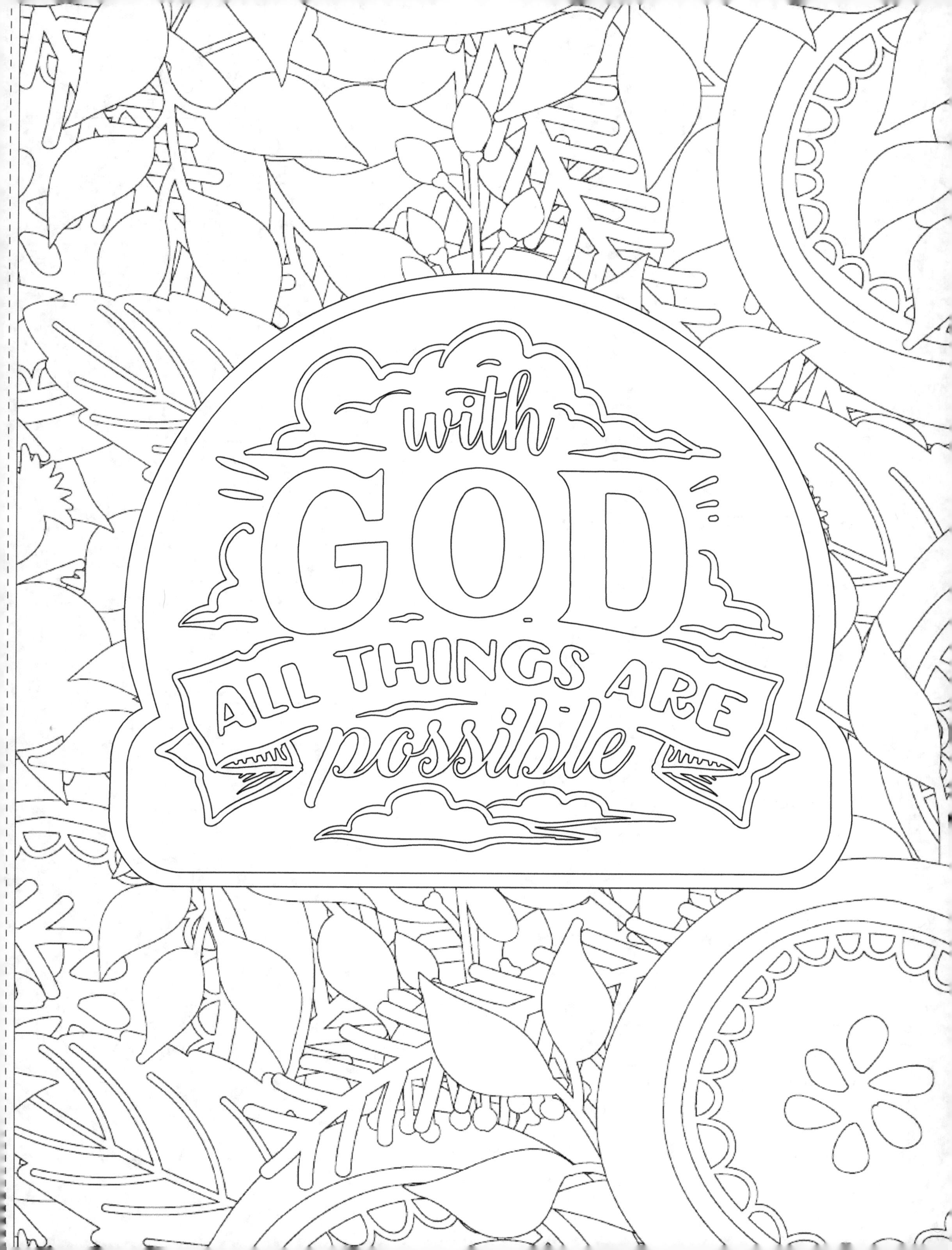

with
GOD
ALL THINGS ARE
possible

September

2021

13 MONDAY

14 TUESDAY

15 WEDNESDAY   Yom Kippur Begins

16 THURSDAY   Yom Kippur Ends

17 FRIDAY

18 SATURDAY

19 SUNDAY

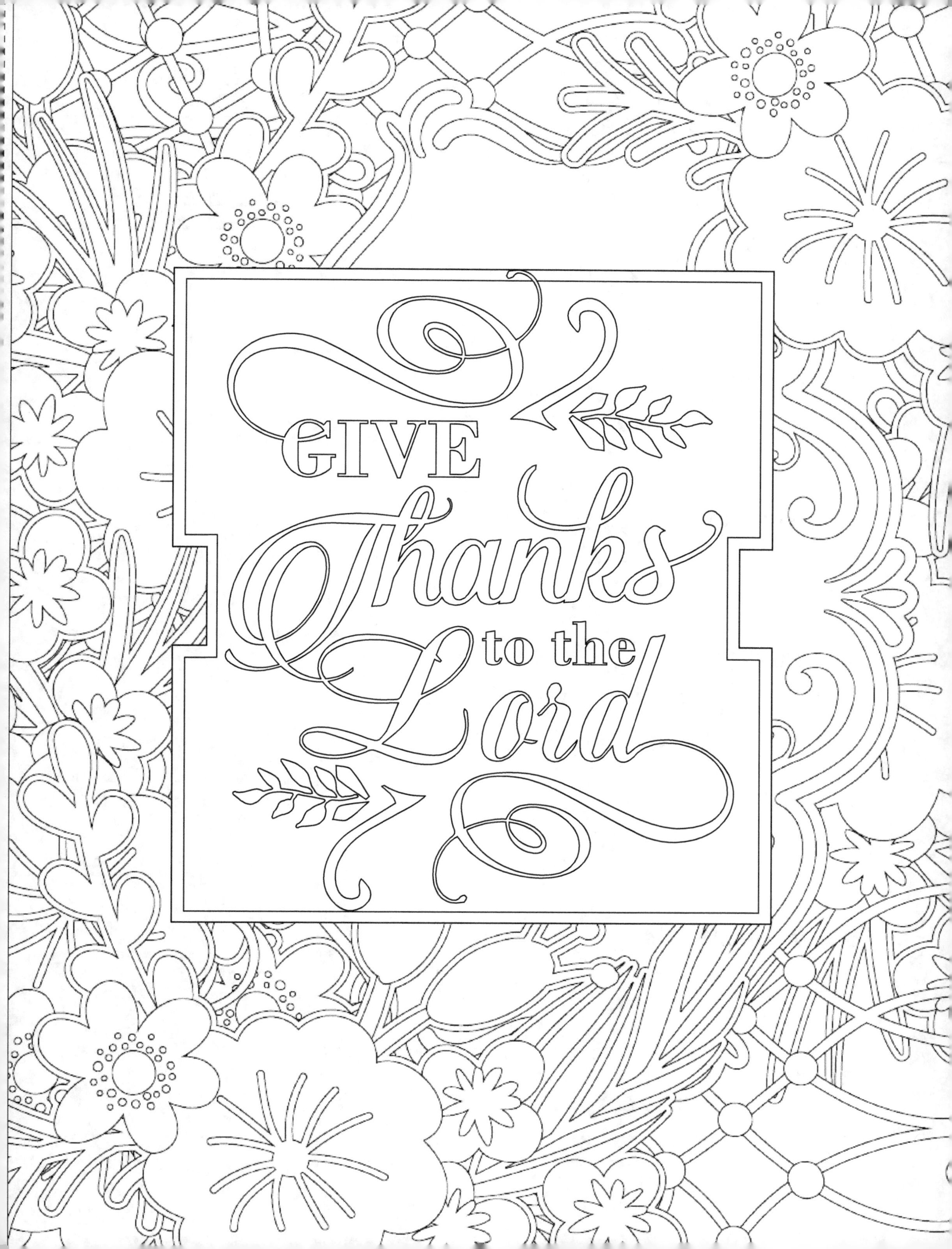
GIVE
Thanks
to the
Lord

September

2021

20 MONDAY

21 TUESDAY

22 WEDNESDAY — First Day of Autumn

23 THURSDAY

24 FRIDAY

25 SATURDAY

26 SUNDAY

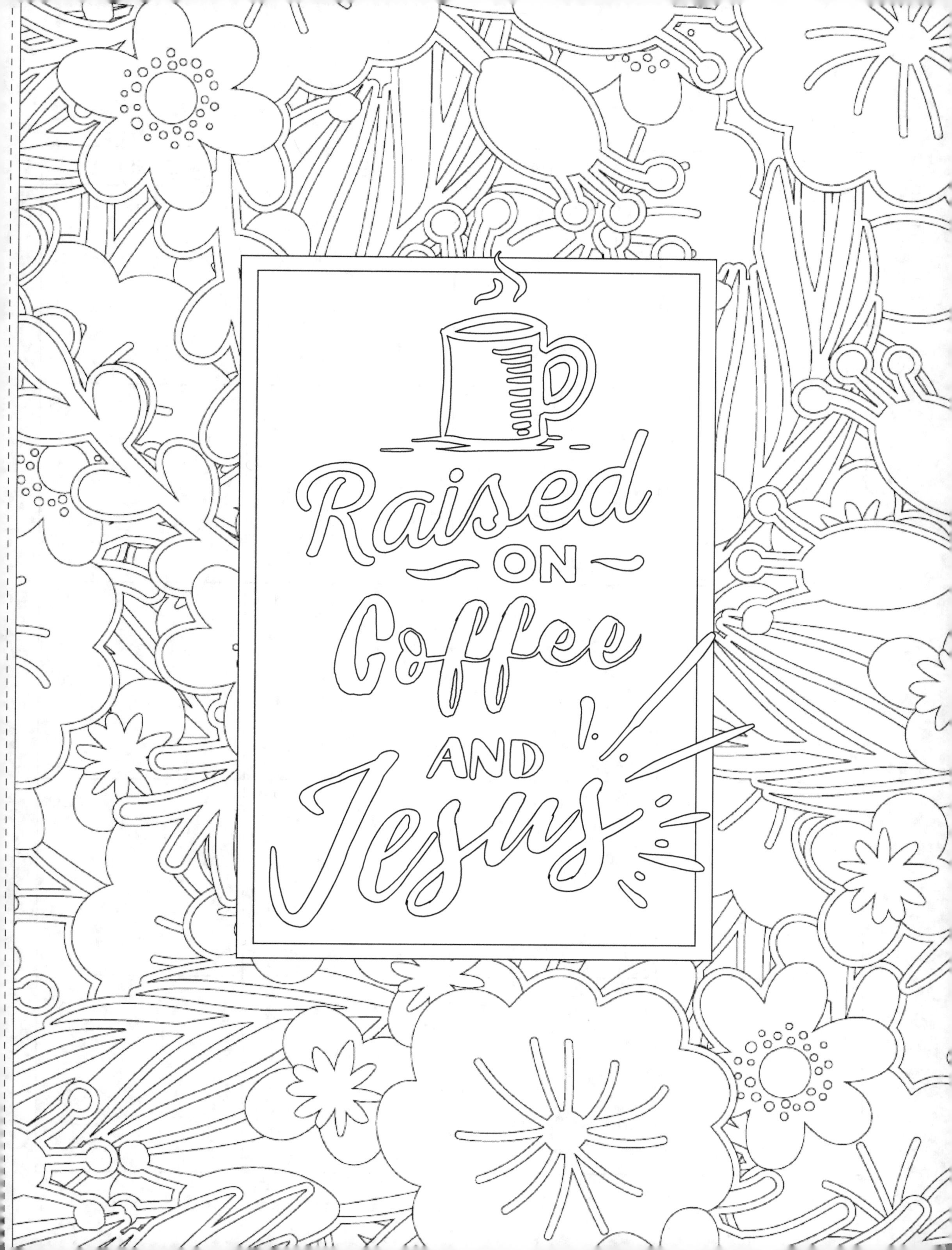
Raised
~ ON ~
Coffee
AND
Jesus

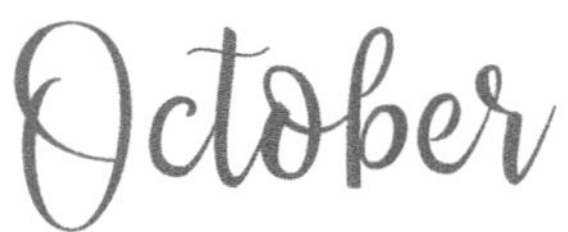

October 2021

SUNDAY	MONDAY	TUESDAY	WEDNESDAY
3	4	5	6
10	11 Indigenous Peoples' Day	12	13
17	18	19	20
24 31 Halloween	25	26	27

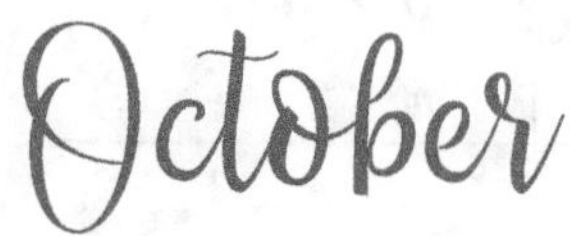

October 2021

THURSDAY	FRIDAY	SATURDAY	NOTES
	1	2	○
			○
			○
			○
			○
7	8	9	○
			○
			○
			○
14	15	16	○
			○
			○
			○
			○
21	22	23	○
			○
			○
			○
			○
28	29	30	NOTES

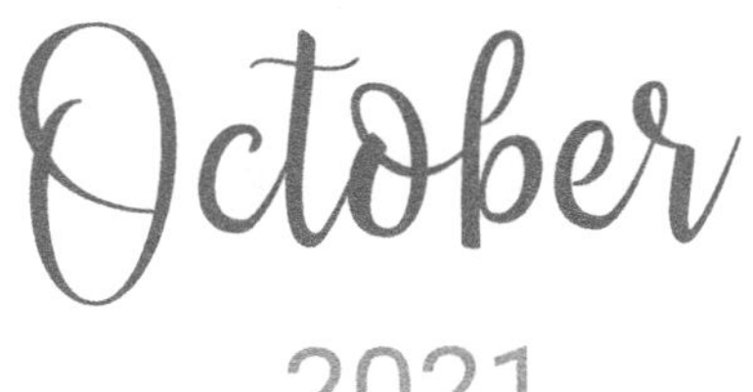

October
2021

October

S M T W T F S
　　　　　1 2
3 4 5 6 7 8 9
10 11 12 13 14 15 16
17 18 19 20 21 22 23
24 25 26 27 28 29 30
31

27 MONDAY

28 TUESDAY

29 WEDNESDAY

30 THURSDAY

01 FRIDAY

02 SATURDAY

03 SUNDAY

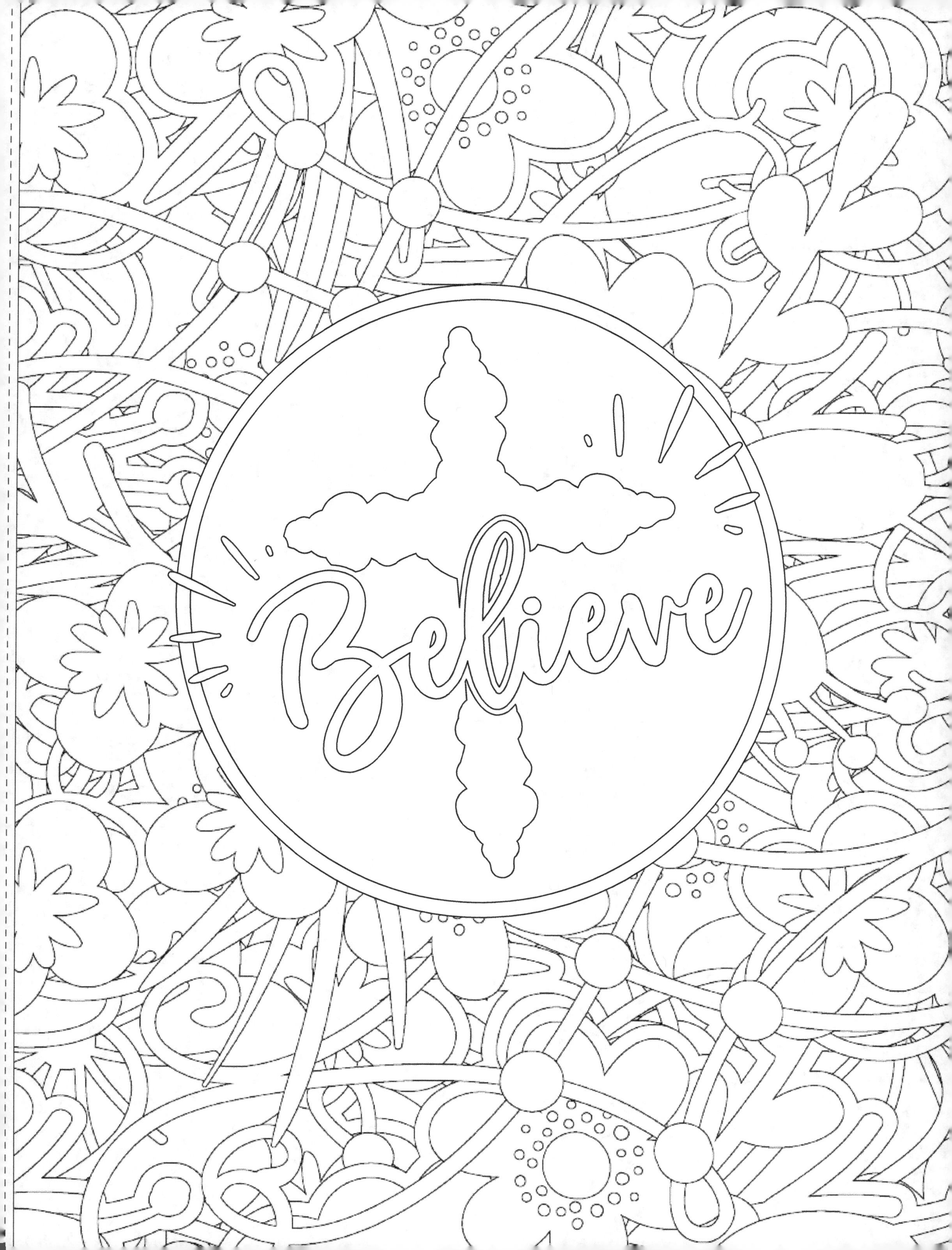
Believe

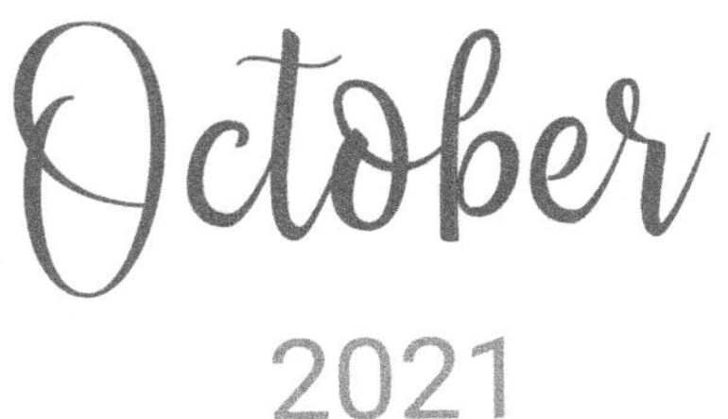

October

2021

<table>
<tr><td colspan="7" align="center">October</td></tr>
<tr><td>S</td><td>M</td><td>T</td><td>W</td><td>T</td><td>F</td><td>S</td></tr>
<tr><td></td><td></td><td></td><td></td><td></td><td>1</td><td>2</td></tr>
<tr><td>3</td><td>4</td><td>5</td><td>6</td><td>7</td><td>8</td><td>9</td></tr>
<tr><td>10</td><td>11</td><td>12</td><td>13</td><td>14</td><td>15</td><td>16</td></tr>
<tr><td>17</td><td>18</td><td>19</td><td>20</td><td>21</td><td>22</td><td>23</td></tr>
<tr><td>24</td><td>25</td><td>26</td><td>27</td><td>28</td><td>29</td><td>30</td></tr>
<tr><td>31</td><td></td><td></td><td></td><td></td><td></td><td></td></tr>
</table>

04 MONDAY

05 TUESDAY

06 WEDNESDAY

07 THURSDAY

08 FRIDAY

09 SATURDAY

10 SUNDAY

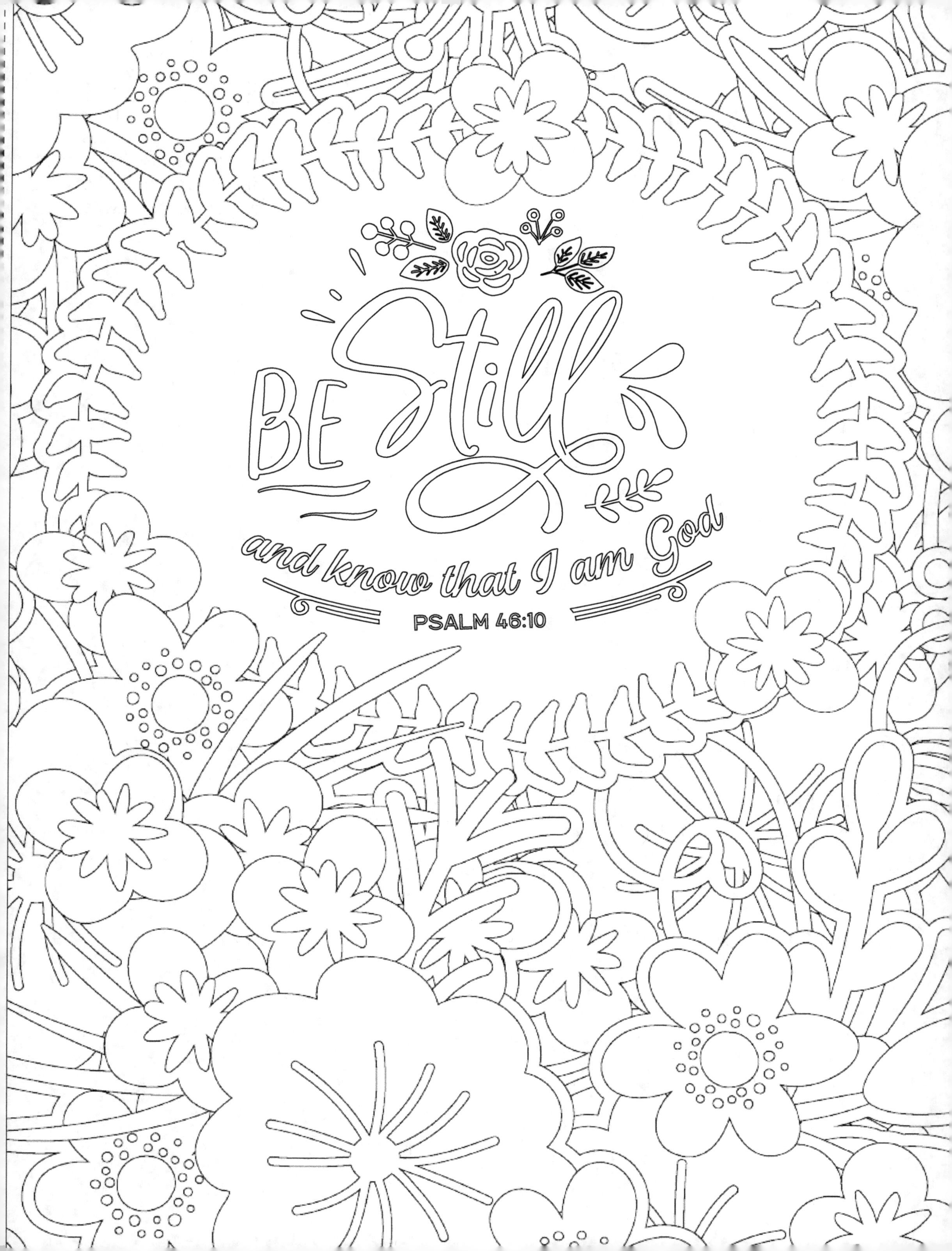

Be Still
and know that I am God
PSALM 46:10

October
2021

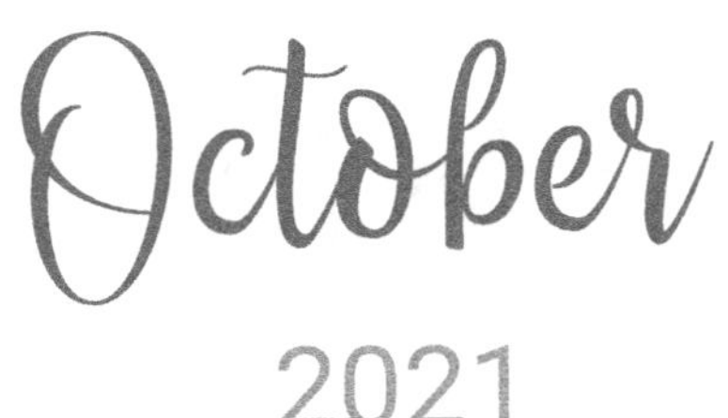

11 MONDAY Indigenous Peoples' Day

12 TUESDAY

13 WEDNESDAY

14 THURSDAY

15 FRIDAY

16 SATURDAY

17 SUNDAY

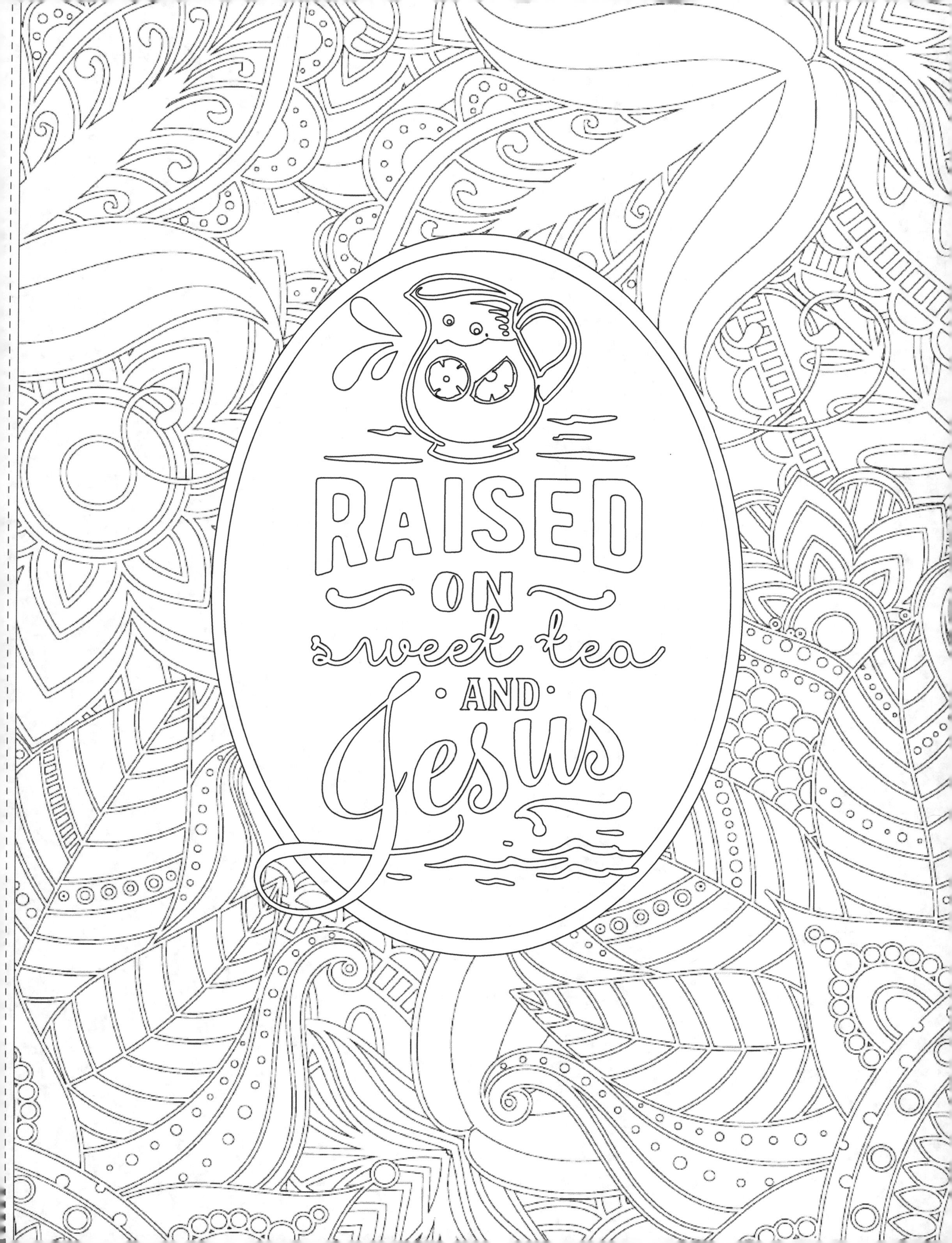

RAISED
ON
sweet tea
AND
Jesus

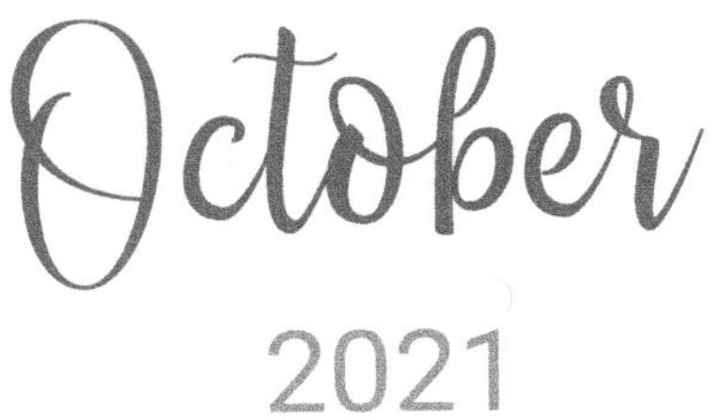

October

2021

18 MONDAY

19 TUESDAY

20 WEDNESDAY

21 THURSDAY

22 FRIDAY

23 SATURDAY

24 SUNDAY

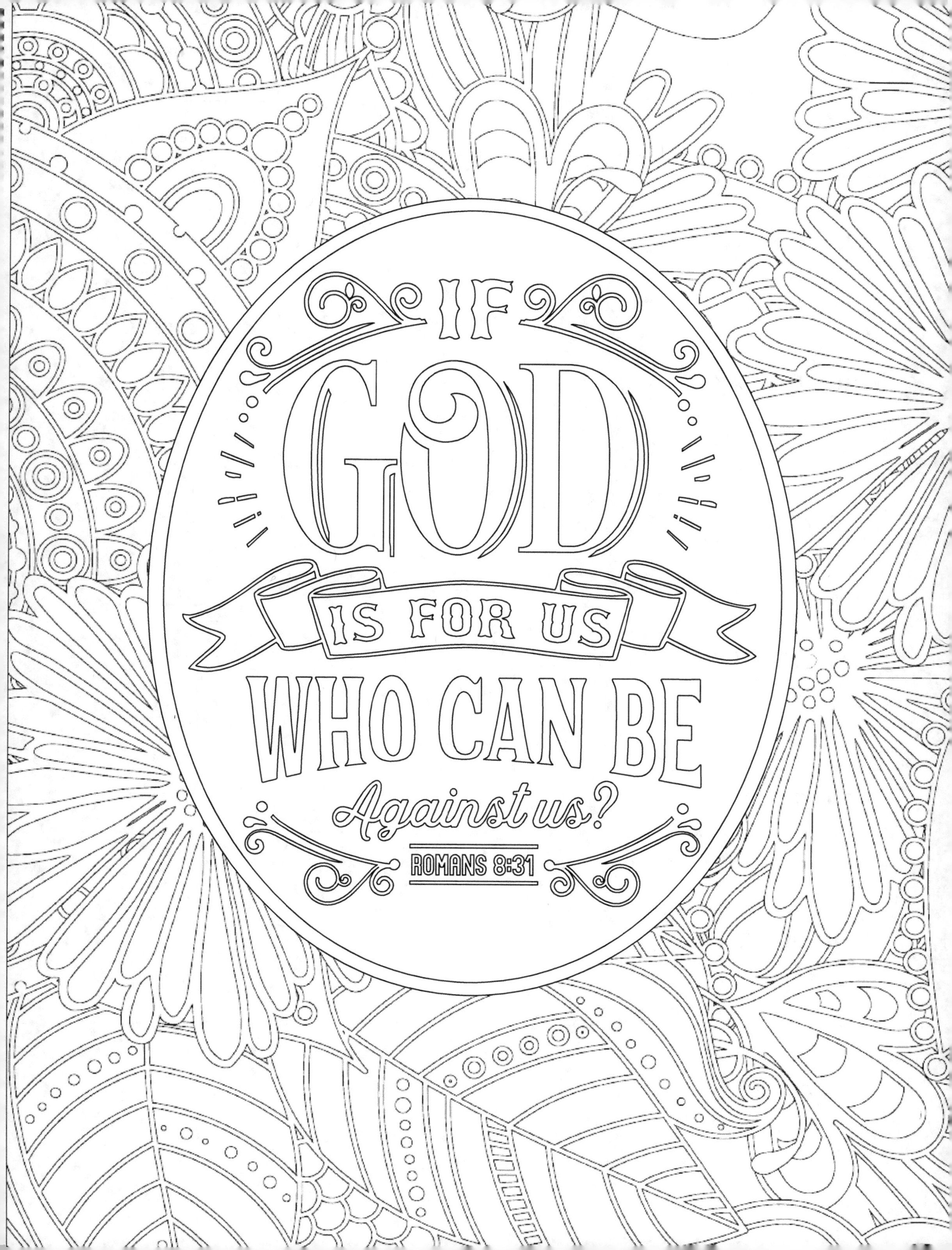

IF
GOD
IS FOR US
WHO CAN BE
Against us?
ROMANS 8:31

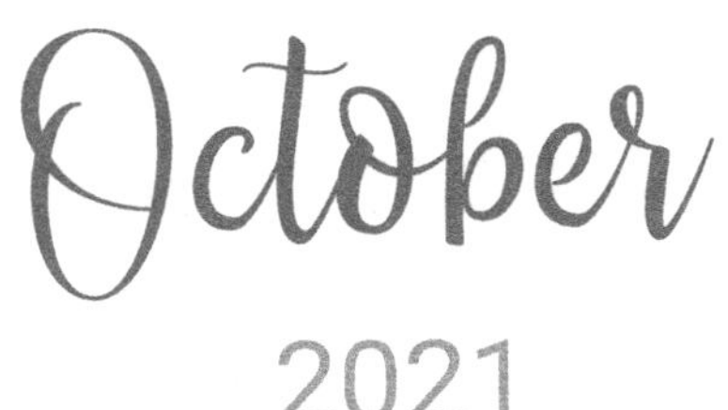

October
2021

25 MONDAY

26 TUESDAY

27 WEDNESDAY

28 THURSDAY

29 FRIDAY

30 SATURDAY

31 SUNDAY Halloween

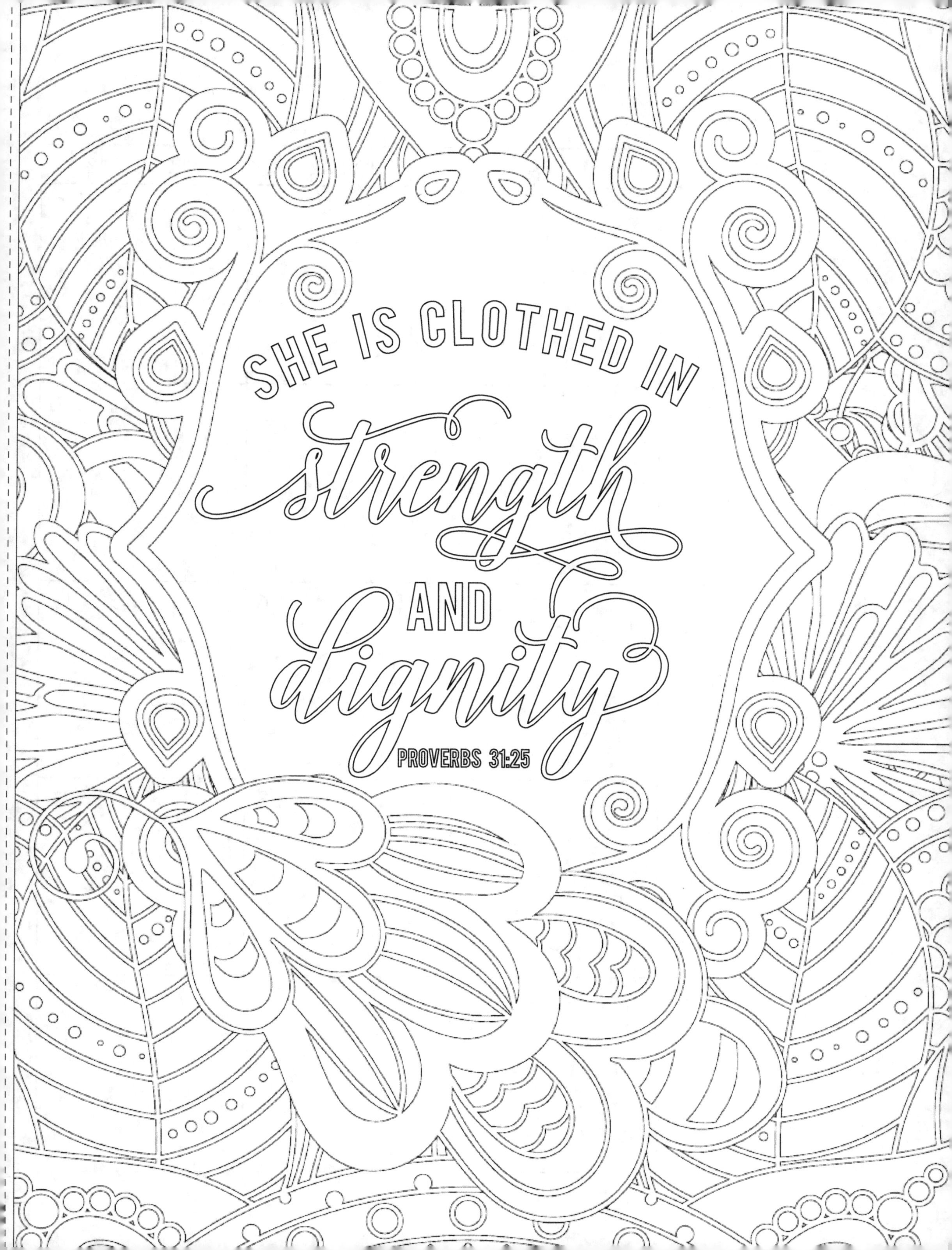

SHE IS CLOTHED IN
strength
AND
dignity
PROVERBS 31:25

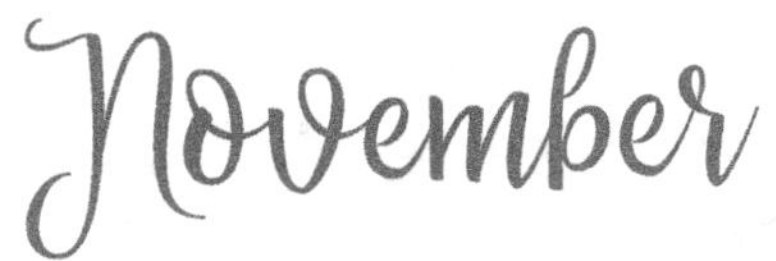

November 2021

SUNDAY	MONDAY	TUESDAY	WEDNESDAY
	1	2	3
7 Daylight Saving Time Ends	8	9	10
14	15	16	17
21	22	23	24
28 Hanukkah Begins	29	30	

November 2021

THURSDAY	FRIDAY	SATURDAY	NOTES
4	5	6	○
			○
			○
			○
			○
11 Veterans Day	12	13	○
			○
			○
			○
18	19	20	○
			○
			○
			○
			○
25 Thanksgiving	26	27	○
			○
			○
			○
			○
			NOTES

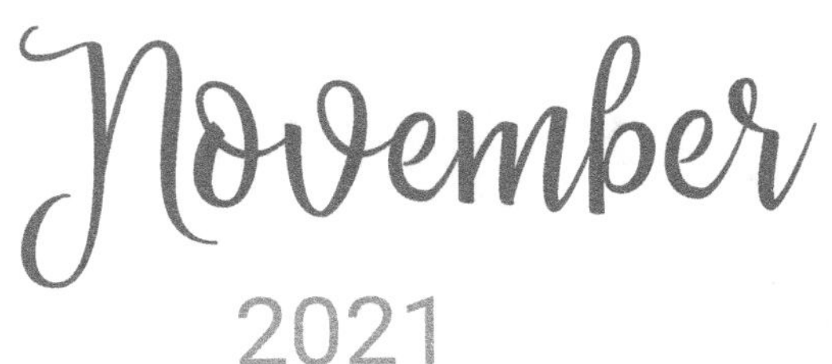

November
2021

01 MONDAY

02 TUESDAY

03 WEDNESDAY

04 THURSDAY

05 FRIDAY

06 SATURDAY

07 SUNDAY   Daylight Saving Time Ends

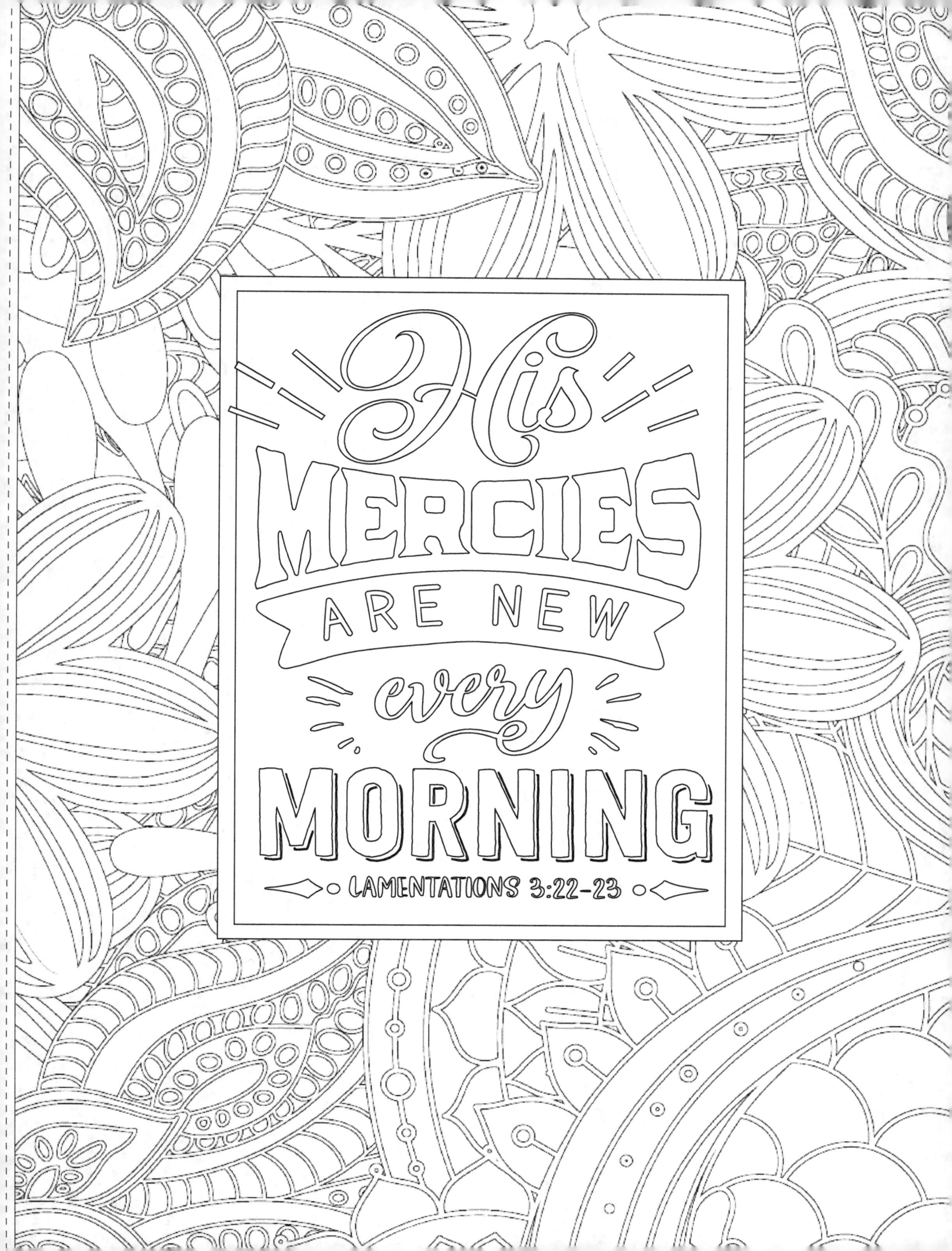
His
MERCIES
ARE NEW
every
MORNING
LAMENTATIONS 3:22-23

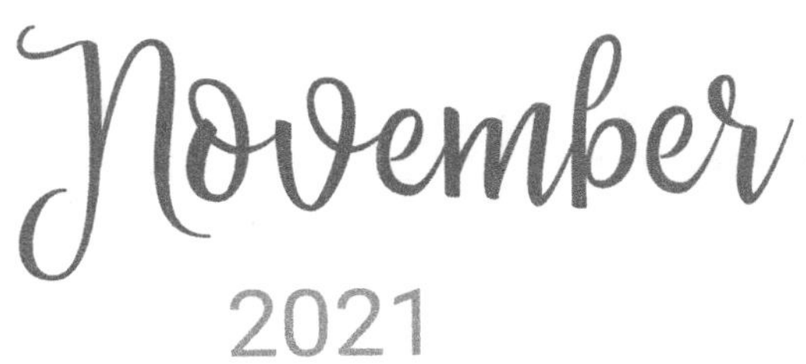

November

2021

08 MONDAY

09 TUESDAY

10 WEDNESDAY

11 THURSDAY   Veterans Day

12 FRIDAY

13 SATURDAY

14 SUNDAY

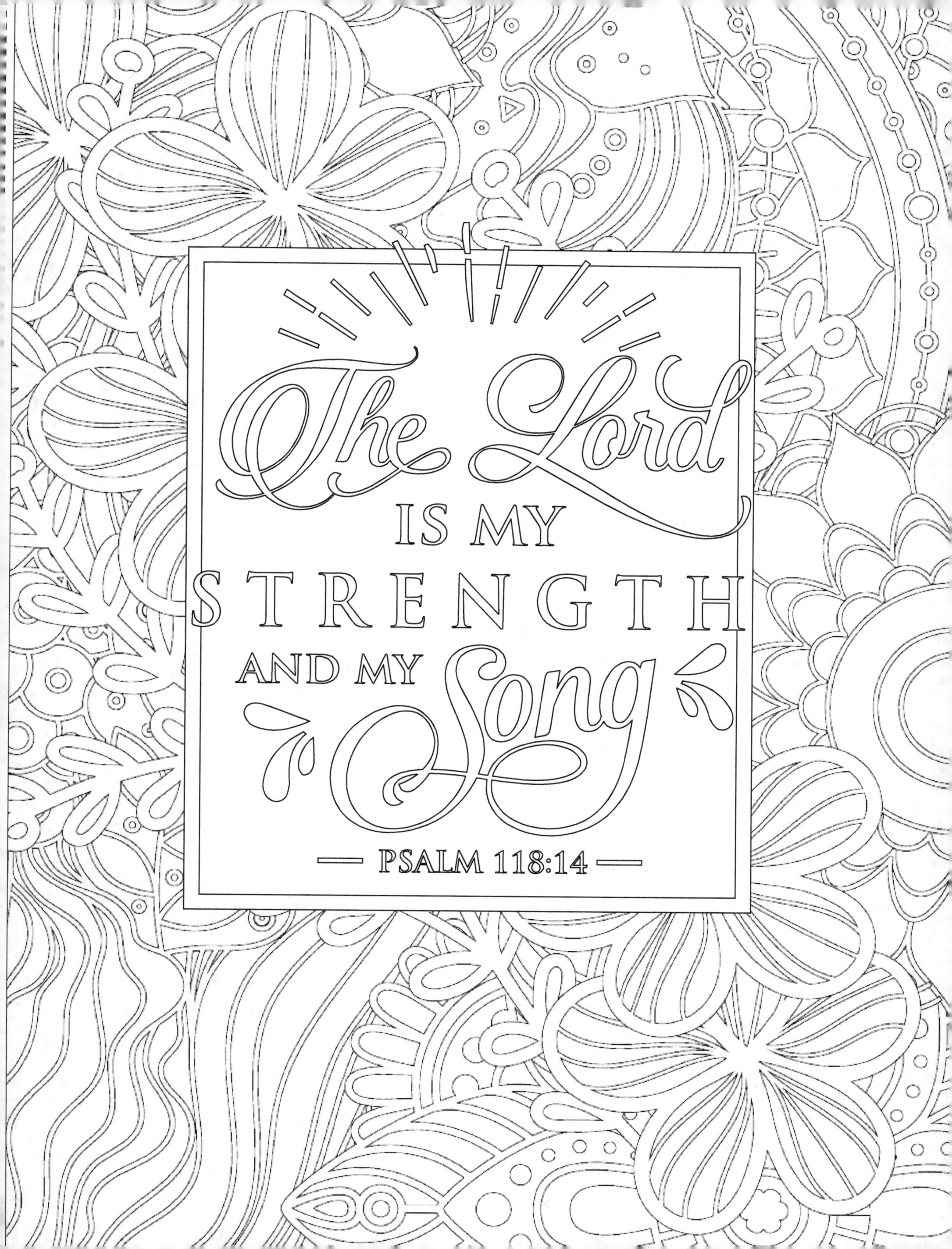

The Lord
IS MY
STRENGTH
AND MY Song
— PSALM 118:14 —

November

2021

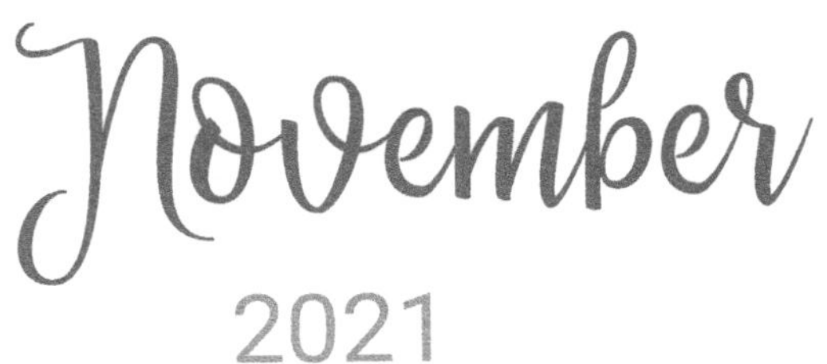

15 MONDAY

16 TUESDAY

17 WEDNESDAY

18 THURSDAY

19 FRIDAY

20 SATURDAY

21 SUNDAY

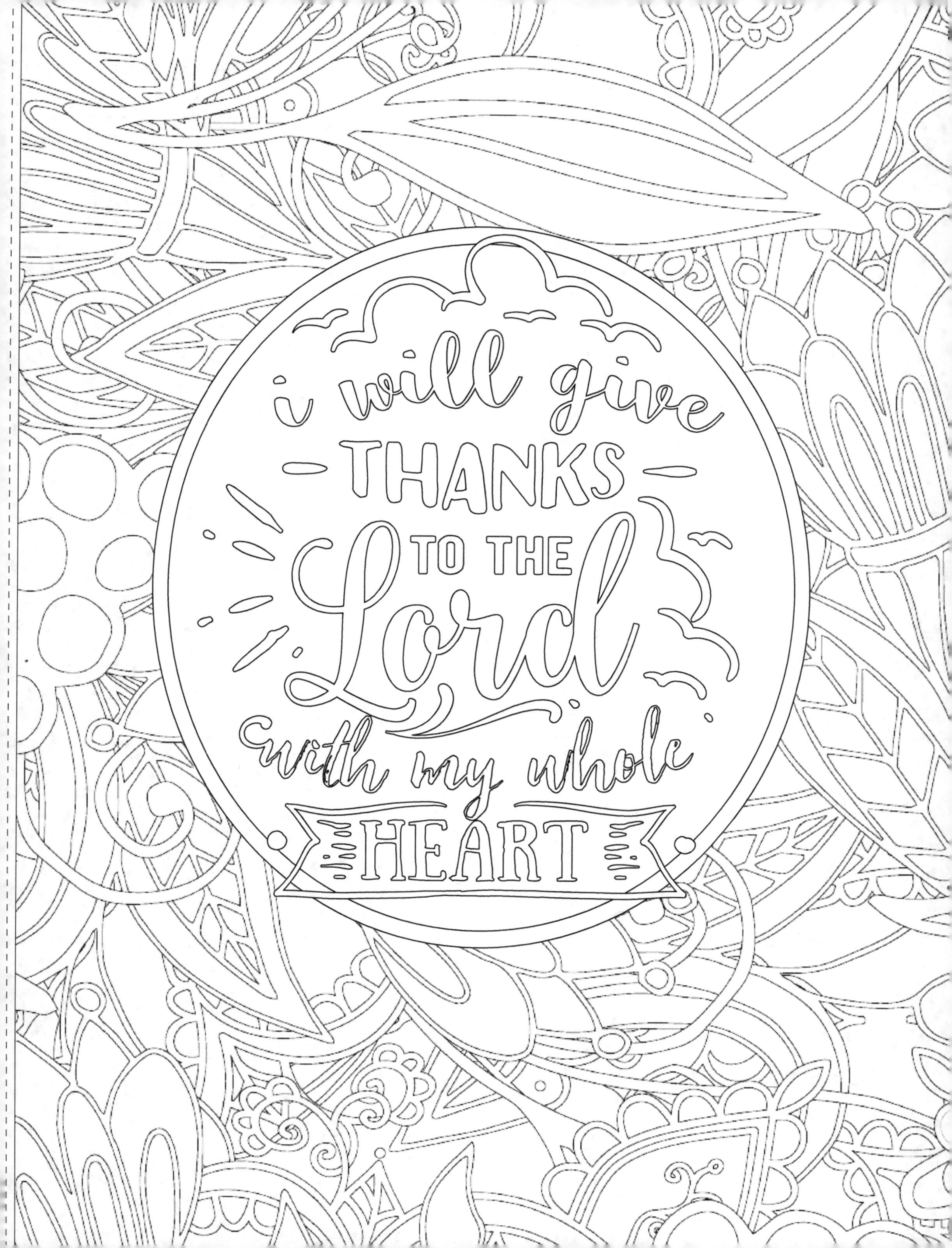

i will give
THANKS
TO THE
Lord
with my whole
HEART

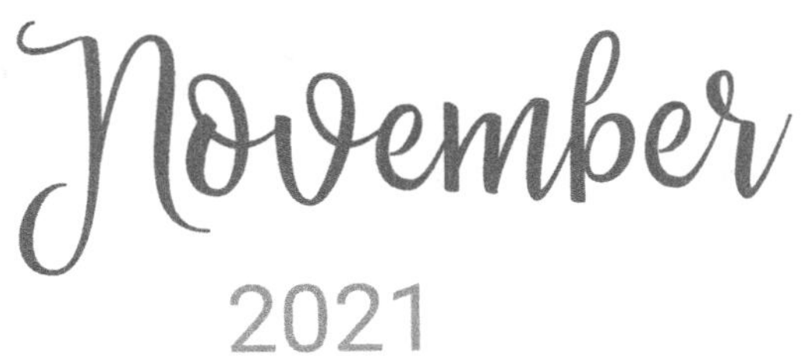

November

2021

22 MONDAY

23 TUESDAY

24 WEDNESDAY

25 THURSDAY   Thanksgiving

26 FRIDAY

27 SATURDAY

28 SUNDAY   Hanukkah Begins

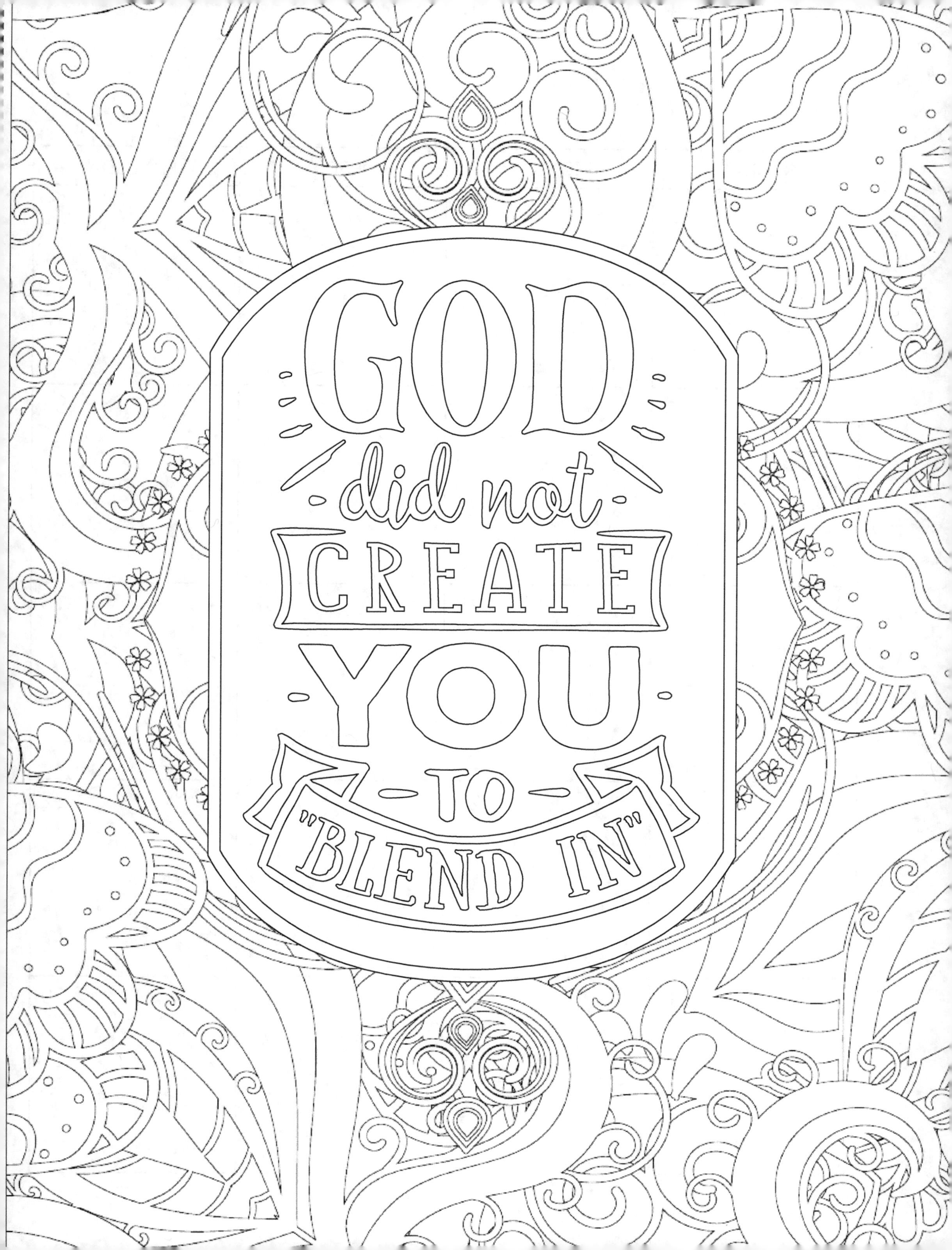
GOD
did not
CREATE
YOU
- TO -
"BLEND IN"

December 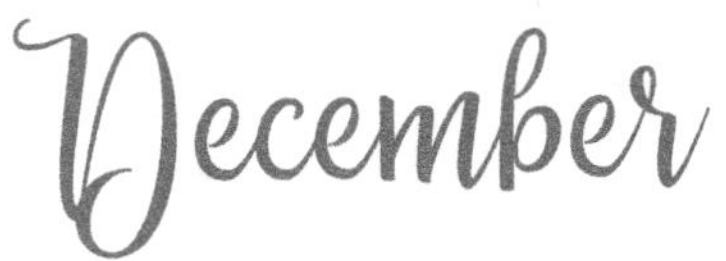 2021

SUNDAY	MONDAY	TUESDAY	WEDNESDAY
			1
5	6 Hanukkah Ends	7	8
12	13	14	15
19	20	21 First Day of Winter	22
26	27	28	29

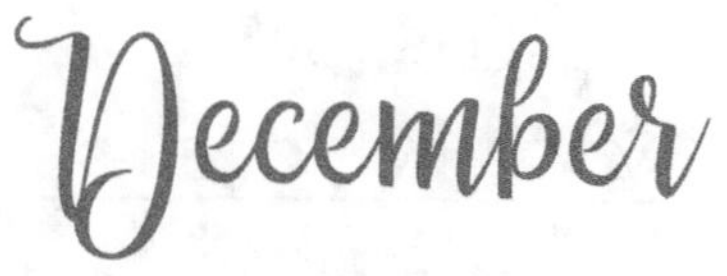

December   2021

THURSDAY	FRIDAY	SATURDAY	NOTES
2	3	4	○
			○
			○
			○
			○
9	10	11	○
			○
			○
			○
16	17	18	○
			○
			○
			○
			○
23	24 Christmas Eve	25 Christmas Day	○
			○
			○
			○
			○
30	31 New Year's Eve		NOTES

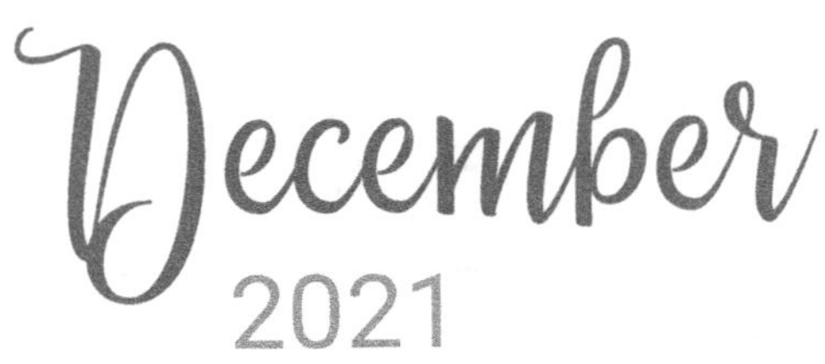

December
2021

29 MONDAY

30 TUESDAY

01 WEDNESDAY

02 THURSDAY

03 FRIDAY

04 SATURDAY

05 SUNDAY

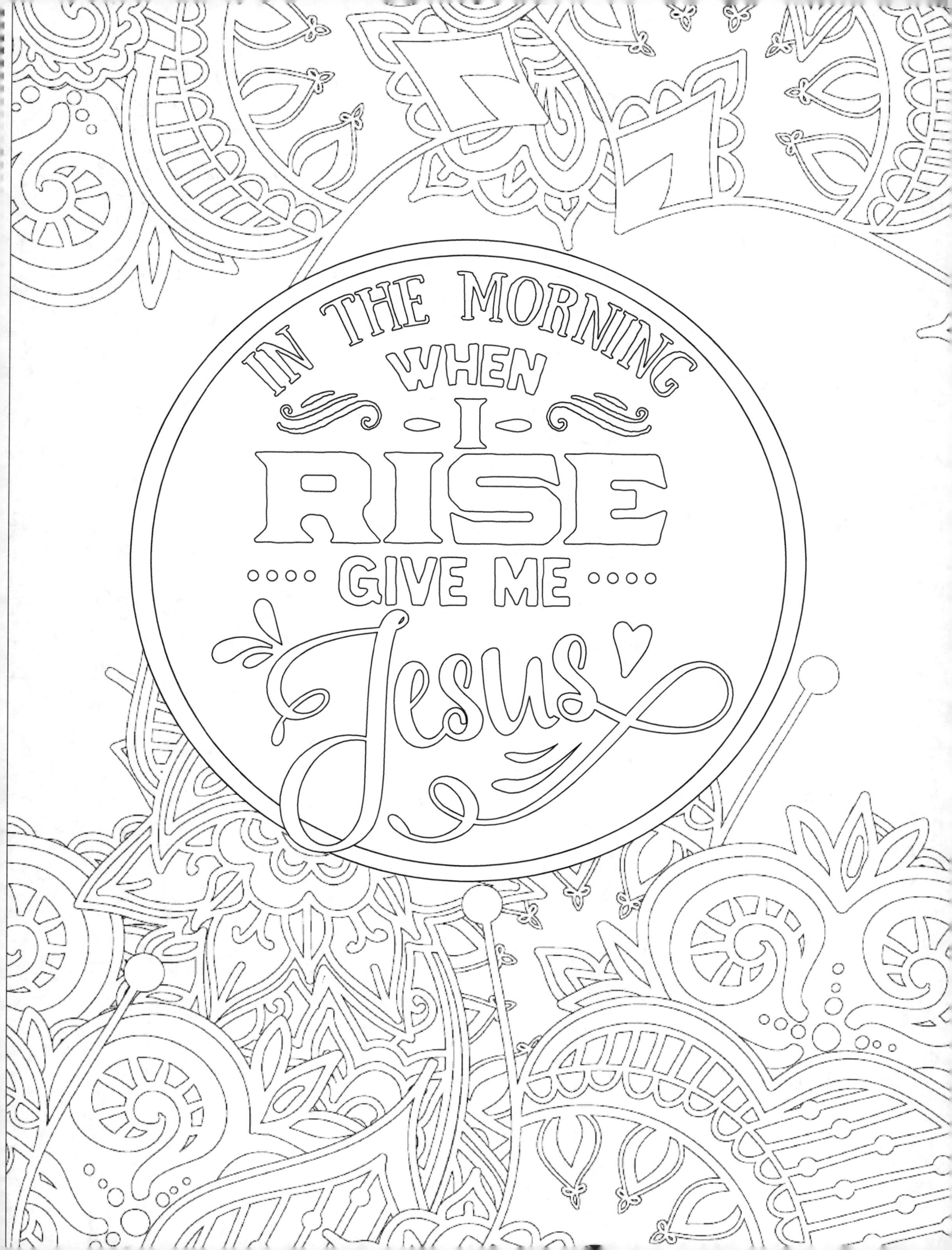

IN THE MORNING
WHEN
-I-
RISE
GIVE ME
Jesus

December
2021

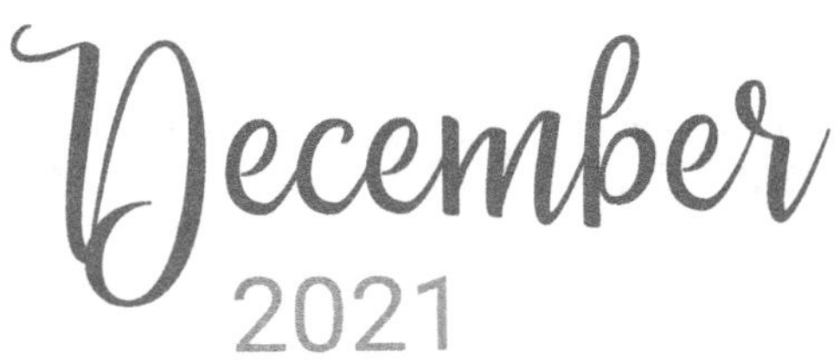

06 MONDAY   Hanukkah Ends

07 TUESDAY

08 WEDNESDAY

09 THURSDAY

10 FRIDAY

11 SATURDAY

12 SUNDAY

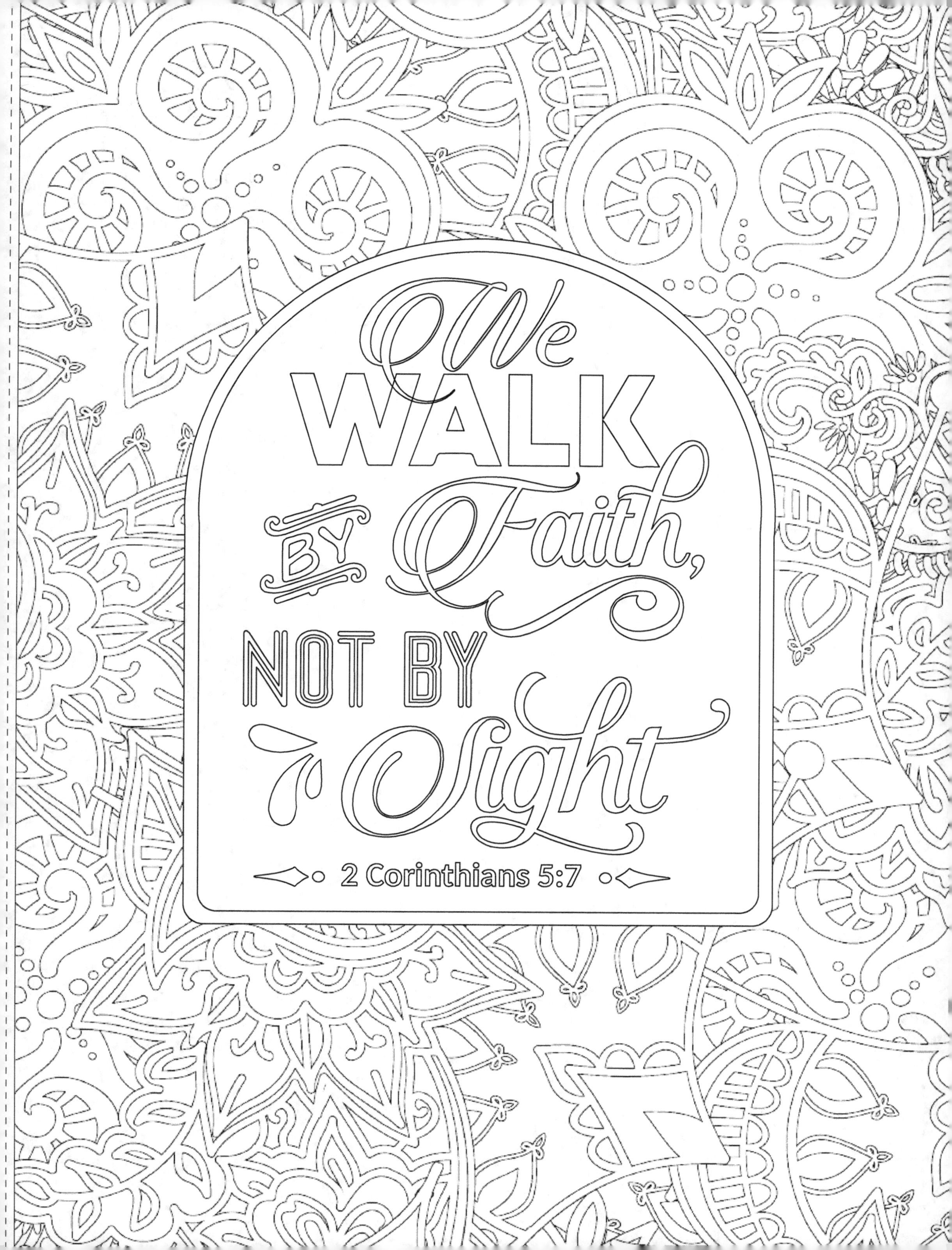

We
WALK
BY Faith,
NOT BY Sight
2 Corinthians 5:7

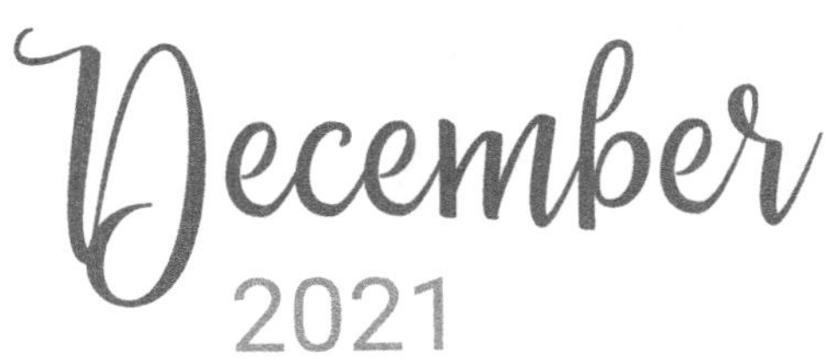

December
2021

13 MONDAY

14 TUESDAY

15 WEDNESDAY

16 THURSDAY

17 FRIDAY

18 SATURDAY

19 SUNDAY

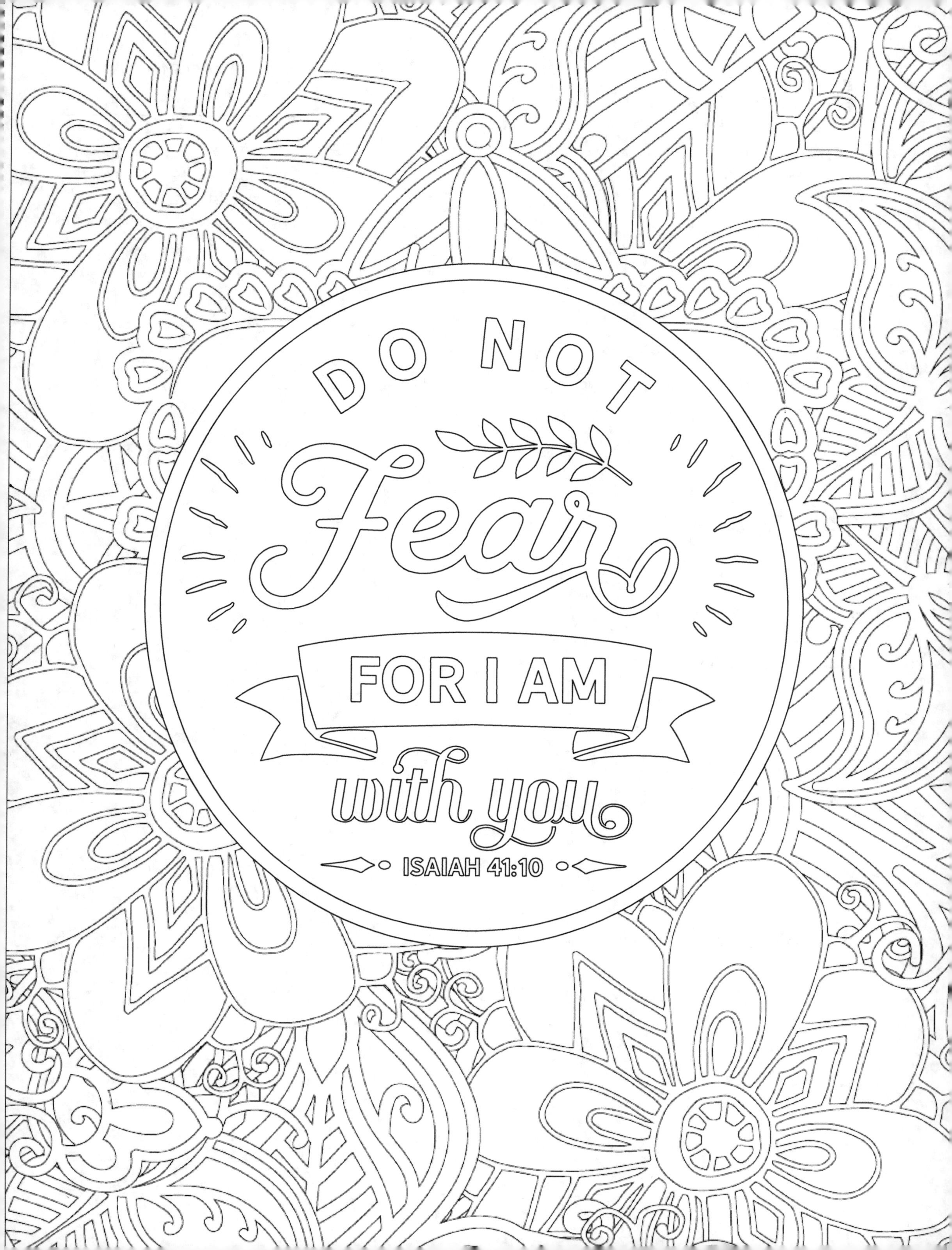

DO NOT
Fear
FOR I AM
with you
ISAIAH 41:10

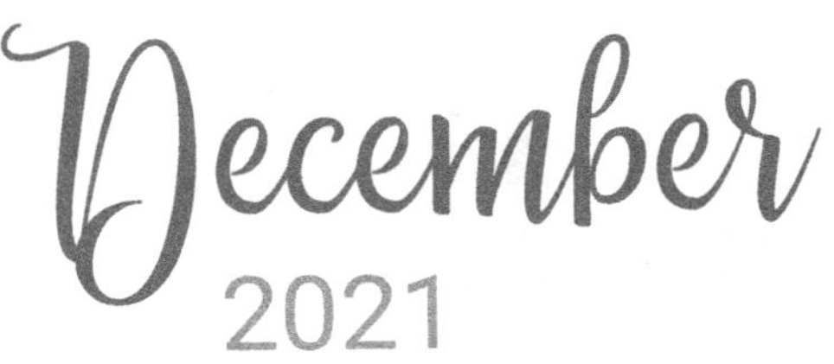

December
2021

20 MONDAY

21 TUESDAY First Day of Winter

22 WEDNESDAY

23 THURSDAY

24 FRIDAY Christmas Eve

25 SATURDAY Christmas Day

26 SUNDAY

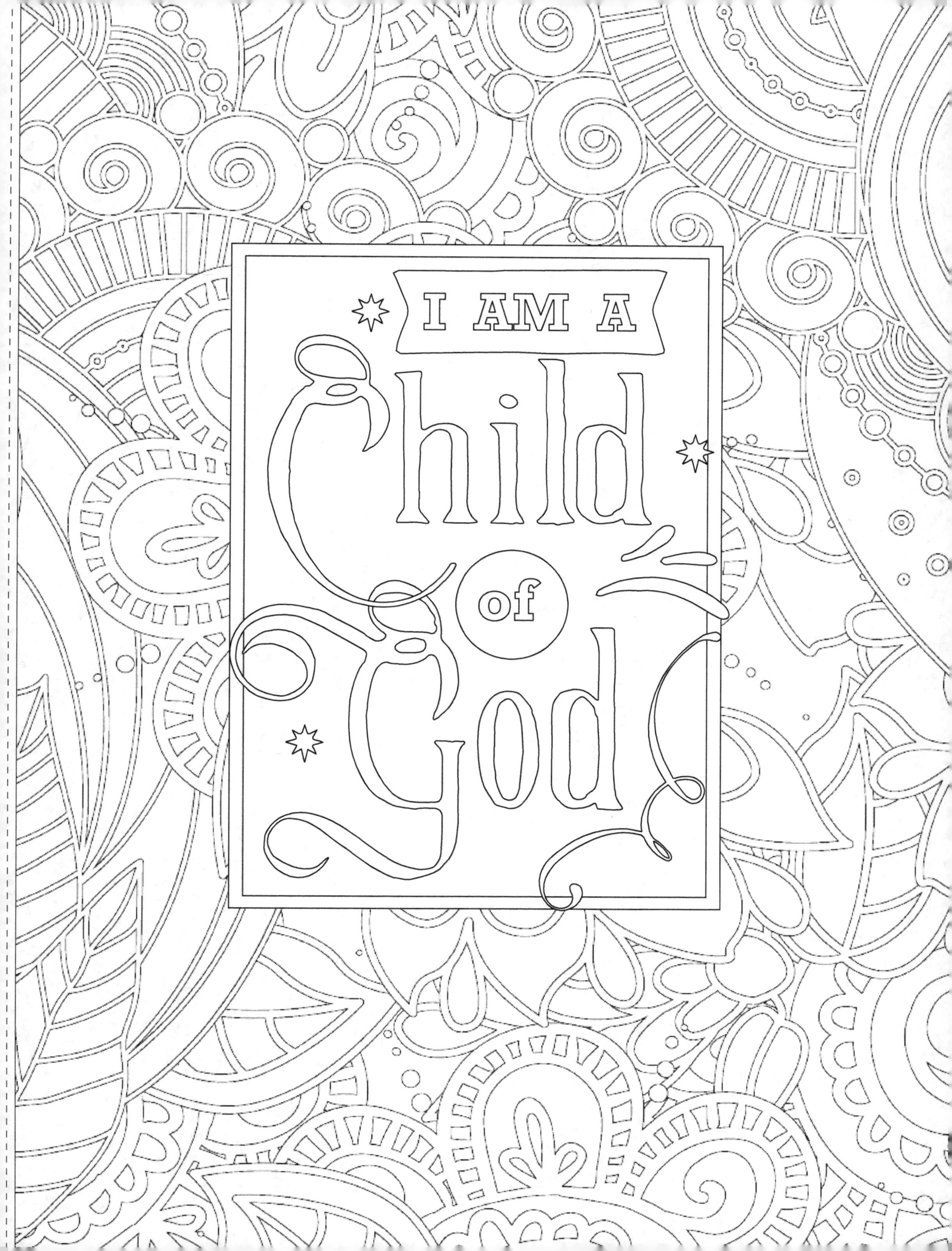

I AM A
Child
of
God

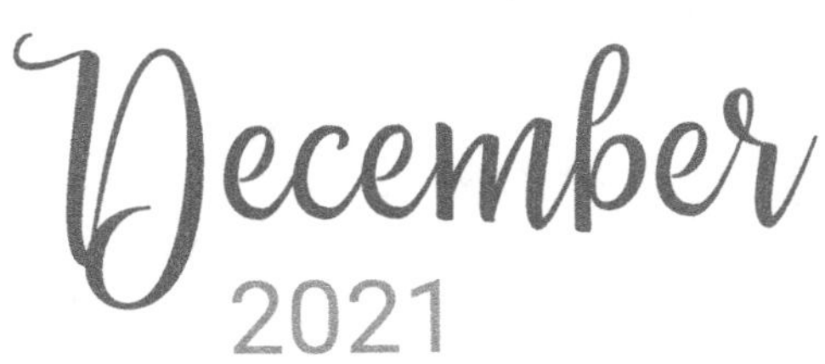

December
2021

27 MONDAY

28 TUESDAY

29 WEDNESDAY

30 THURSDAY

31 FRIDAY   New Year's Eve

01 SATURDAY   New Year's Day

02 SUNDAY

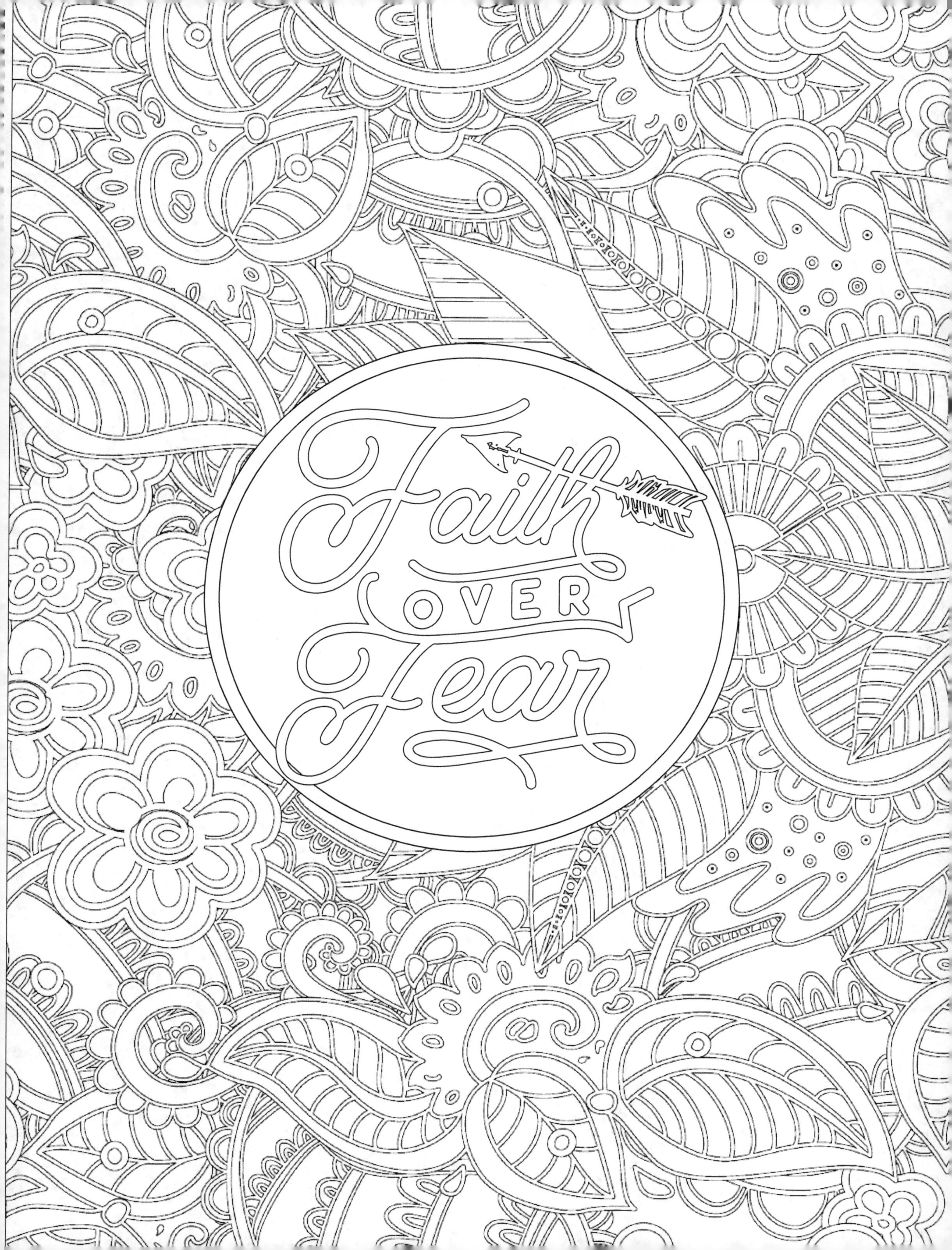

Faith
OVER
Fear